INSPIRED
MESSAGES
OF
TRUTH
EDUCATION
FOR
TRANSFORMATION

WILLIE JAMES WEBB

Theological Ethicist

INDEPENDENTLY PUBLISHED BY: WILLIE JAMES WEBB

TABLE OF CONTENTS

INTRODUCTION   1
CHAPTER 2
Human Disorders and Cultural Dysfunctions   4
CHAPTER 3
Blessings of God   59
CHAPTER 4
The Generosity of God   72
CHAPTER 5
Standards Set By God   83
CHAPTER 6
Duties of God's People   91
CHAPTER 7
Black American Salvation Values   105
CHAPTER 8
The Vital Priority of Education   115
CHAPTER 9
Salvation In Jesus Christ   141
CHAPTER 10
Theological Ethics   151
CHAPTER 11
Goals and Themes of Public Theology   165
CHAPTER 12
The Mission of the Gospel   204

INTRODUCTION

The messages of this book are truly inspired by the Spirit, Truth and Word of God. This inspiration from God is an inspiration of enlightenment to perceive and understand the precarious predicament of the people of God in America and the earth in this intricate technological age of the 21st Century. It is an inspiration that seeks answers through the Words, Ways and Will of God.

The receptivity and response to this inspiration of God is an openness and a desire for answers, solutions, guidance and directions for the Will of God to reveal the answers to a culture in crisis and confusion. What is the diagnosis of this pervasive human hatred? What are the answers to the growing problems of crime and violence? What are the answers to political corruption, cultural confusion and social violence? What are the reasons for unsound doctrines, destructive ideologies, proliferations of indoctrination, anti-life, anti-Bible, anti-God, anti-Christ, anti-America? These are questions that gave rise to the inspired messages of this book. What are the answers to these unsustainable problems and questions?

God has blessed humanity with the answers to these serious, lethal and unsustainable problems. God has blessed humanity with the reality of truth, the light of enlightenment, knowledge, wisdom, understanding, the Holy Bible and a Savior in Jesus Christ. God has given mankind spiritual discernment. These blessings enable mankind to discern that which is good, merciful and pleasing in the Will, the Word and in the sight of God.

Therefore, man is capable of determining that which is good, just, beautiful and loving. Based on these gifts God has provided man with four branches of knowledge to determine and validate the reality of truth. Someone has said, "Truth is that stability which underlies the transitory processes of the universe!" The four distinct branches of knowledge that God has blessed man with are Science, Art, Law and Theology. Through these four branches of knowledge, man can relate objectively and with purpose to God and God's creation. These are the four branches of knowledge of degrees that are granted by universities of higher education.

This book, Inspired Messages of Truth, is based on the foundations of Public Theology through the proper utilization of Science, Art, Law and Theology.

The basis of America's and humanity's cultural crisis can be analyzed through the scientific, artistic, legalistic and theistical abuses and dysfunctions.

Specifically, the cultural crisis is related to mankind's Ignorance of these four branches of knowledge: their misuse and abuse of these four branches of knowledge. When these four branches of knowledge, individually or collectively; are not known, ignored, or improperly used or abused, they precipitate problems and crises in the human enterprise.

These four branches of knowledge; known as Science, Art, Law and Theology, are utilized by public theology. Public theology has the capability of diagnosing and defining the human dysfunctionalities in our persons, families, institutions, societies and nations. Public theology is the Truth of God for the public practice in the public domain of society. In addition to diagnosing human and social problems, public theology has the capability of providing the appropriate prescriptions and treatment plans for resolutions and restoration.

There are many familiar inspired messages in this book that are relevant to many individuals, groups, institutions and nations. I hope that these inspired messages will be utilized, taught, recited and shared abroad.

These messages of inspiration will not only motivate victorious living but will provide a wide range of noble things to accomplish, along with the expertise on how to do them well. This book reveals the causes of our cultural crisis along with their cures, remedies and resolutions. This book of inspired messages of truth provides the essential knowledge and guidelines for the practice of public theology. There is more than enough information to begin the sacred work of transforming the lethal tide of destruction into building God's Kingdom on Earth as it is in Heaven. LET US BEGIN NOW!

W.J. Webb
Pastoral Ethicist

CHAPTER 2
HUMAN DISORDERS AND CULTURAL DYSFUNCTIONS

There are specific reasons and traceable rational causes for social and cultural dysfunctions in American society. The identification of these social and cultural dysfunctions provides a glimmer of hope that they can be arrested and reversed. These dysfunctions are not mysterious. There exist rational reasons, and natural causes in an identifiable social, cultural, moral, ethical and spiritual human interactive environment. The dysfunctional components can be identified, analyzed, evaluated and prognosticated.

The conditions and components below are provided to make possible prescriptions for resolutions, solutions and remedies for the abatement of the serious American culture crisis:

Precipitating Conditions for the American Culture Crisis

1. The absence and silence of the Church in the public square.
2. The pious privatized priestly religion behind the stained glass and veiled walls in retreat from the general society.
3. The retreat of the Church and clergy from the raging spiritual wickedness and ideological warfare.

4. The unchecked and unchallenged rampant proliferation of unsound doctrines, invalid principles, unjust laws and partisan politics.
5. The exclusion of biblical knowledge and spiritual values from public education.
6. The exclusion of the spiritual domain of learning from public education. (Restricting public education to the cognitive, affective and psychomotor domains is a serious detriment to the moral, ethical and spiritual development of children).
7. The open rebellion against God-ordained creation, truth, divine laws, natural laws and sovereign authority.
8. Misguided cultism, sectarianism, ecumenism, cultural diversity and religious pluralism.
9. Increasing moral relativity, ethical neutrality and uncivilized standards with no spiritual guidance or moral compass.
10. Increasing secularism that ignores God, Jesus Christ, spiritual values, truth and justice.
11. Increasing alienation from the traditional values of Judea-Christian, Declaration of Independence, U. S. Constitution, family values of marriage between a man and a woman, patriotism for the Country and one Nation Under God.
12. Refusal to seek or consider rational objective and authoritative scientific and theological truth regarding the origin, classification, social role and the most appropriate, humane and ethical adaptation, accommodation and assimilation of LGBT persons into the synchronized human fabric of society. What is the sustaining humane, ethical, moral and legal

balance for the best interest of LGBT persons and the society at large?

13. The social autonomous movements that include, "Political identity", "Gender Equality," "Me To," "Toxic Traditional Masculinity, Transgender Restroom Use," "Fluid Sex Identity," "Black Lives Matter," "Same-Sex Adoptions," "Women's Movement," "LGBT Rights VS Religious Liberty," etc. What about the human family?

14. The negligence of families, churches, schools, community institutions and government agencies of not providing, as a needed priority, Character education and Judeo-Christian values for their children. (Judeo-Christian values are universal human values and are inclusive of the Old and New Testaments).

Continued, Precipitating Conditions for Culture Crisis

15. The transition of public schools into tax-supported charter schools adopts various standards and values for the common good or for the national interest. Their traditional standards and values are being diminished by the private profit industrial complex greed. Quality and comprehensive student education is no longer the priority. It is education for monetary profit and greed. The commonalities for civilized human unity and national pride are being eliminated in the tax-supported charter schools.

16. There is an abandonment or failure to adopt hope for the future, dreams, visions, goals, future orientation and plans for personal success on the part of vast numbers of students and other young Americans.

Excessive unmotivated and uninspired people create excessive failure identities and social problems.

17. The selfish, self-centered indulgence to sensate pleasures and destructive addictions to drugs, technology, harmful habits and hatred abound without elevated ethical and moral values that focus on meaningful purpose and significant goals in life.

18. There are widespread fears, reluctance and confusion about growing up to be a man or woman with maturity and responsibility to develop to the optimum their God-given talents and potential to face the future with confidence and courage.

19. In a society where unsound doctrines, unethical practices and immoral standards are accepted, tolerated and even promoted, how can any person, and especially the young, find their way to acceptable standards, sound doctrines and the truth?

20. A most serious and dangerous cultural dysfunction is when a divided government fails to follow its Constitution, uses taxpayers' money and resources to wage political partisan wars within the government and infiltrates and weaponizes government agencies to harm and destroy selected American groups and individual Americans.

IT IS URGENT THAT THESE PRECIPITATING
CONDITIONS FOR CULTURE CRISES BE CORRECTED!

The Christian Institute of Public Theology
Atlanta, Georgia

HUMAN DISORDERS ARE DERIVED FROM CULTURAL CONDITIONS
Cultural Conditions Can be Changed

-The Public Theologian-

SOME CONDITIONS THAT IMPACT THE CULTURAL CRISIS

1. Lack of biblical education, knowledge and reverence to God the Creator. Subsequently, the infiltration of atheistic ideological influences throughout the American culture.
2. The failure to transmit traditional biblical, ethical, moral, spiritual and patriotic values to the youth and the general society. We must transmit these values to our children:
3. The lack of youth-oriented ethical, moral, artistic, spiritual and cultural enrichment training in the home, school, Church and community. Public theology must lead.
4. The failure of the Church and the educational institutions to teach boldly and with authority, the primary purpose of life and the roles of men, women, husbands, wives and children according to traditional biblical standards. Public theology can lead the way.
5. The failure of the Church and ecclesiastical leaders to set the patterns for ethical, moral, patriotic, professional, civilized and humane standards for the general society.

6. There is an increasing moral relativity (no distinction between right and wrong), and ethical neutrality (no stand for right or wrong) in present-day American society.

7. Dehumanizing and divisive personal and political identities disassociated from the Human Family and the Household of God. We are people of God, First and foremost.

8. There is a growing secularism that seeks to eliminate God, Jesus Christ and biblical influence and symbols from the American society and culture. This must be reversed.

9. Spiritual demoralization is pervading American society with a loss of faith and hope in God. People are surrendering to helplessness, hopelessness, despair and defeat.

10. There is pervasive sexual misuse, abuse and gender role confusion. There are diminished traditional family values of child-rearing, family cohesion and public responsibility.

11. There is increasing denial, distortion and demonization of the reality of validated truth in society and public life. There is even hostility. against truth and traditional values.

12. Merit systems are being eliminated. Judicial systems are dysfunctional. The required due process of law by the US Constitution is being routinely violated. Can be changed.

-THE PUBLIC THEOLOGIANS MUST LEAD THE WAY IN TRANSFORMING CORRUPT CULTURES-

REBELLIOUS DERANGEMENT SPIRITS AGAINST GOD

Revelatory Expressions of Ignorance and Evil
(The People of God)

1. The Mockery of God, the Bible and the Christian Faith.
2. Ignores Evil and the Destruction of Sin.
3. Practice with Impunity Known Established Deviant Behaviors.
4. Makes Blatant Choices of Evil in the Presence of Goodness.
5. Ignores the validated Truth of Science, Art, Law and Theology.
6. Disrespects and Disparages Openly, the Stark Reality of Truth.
7. Maliciously Relativizes Absolute Truth.
8. Destigmatizes Immorality, Sin and Evil.
9. Normalizes Mental Disorders and Pathological Behaviors.
10. Normalizes Moral Depravities, Unethical Behavior & Illegal Violations.
11. Normalizes the Practice of Pathological Abnormalities.
12. Blatant Denial of Scientific Factual Reality.
13. Normalizes Secularism, Criminality and Insanity.
14. Makes a Mockery of Human Nature Created by God.
15. Chooses Wicked Deviations from Civilized Standards.
16. Embraces and Practice Immoral Regressive Degeneration of Civilization.

17. Substitutes the Demonic Antithesis of Civilized Values of Life.
18. Rejects the Way of Life for the Wicked Descent into Damnation & Death.
19. Works Against Life and Salvation for Death and Damnation.
20. Represents the Evil Fruits of Hatred, Idolatry and wickedness.
21. Embraces Decisions and Choices to Deceive Humanity & Reject God.
22. Rejects the Ways of Love and Life for the Ways of Evil and Death.
23. Rejects Knowledge & Wisdom and Choose to be Ignorant and a Fool.
24. Misuse, Abuse and Exploits the Values of Life for Darkness and Death.
25. Preys on the Weak, Naive and Innocent for Filthy Gain & Sick Pleasure.
26. Consumed with Selfishness, Human Disregard, Hatred and Absurdities.
27. Hell Bent Rebellion Against God, Truth, Knowledge, Love and Life.
28. Pre-occupied with Deceiving, Misleading, Mistreating and Cheating.
29. Mislead the Youth before They can Read and Meet Their Basic Needs.
30. Turn Ye, Turn Ye from Your Evil Ways; For Why will Ye Die..? (EZ 33:11)
31. My People are Destroyed for Lack of Knowledge. (Hosea 4:6)
32. Call on the Name of the Lord and be Saved. (Acts:21)
33. Beloved, believe not every Spirit, but Try the Spirits... (1 John 4:1)

Consequences of Sin and Violation of God's Laws
(The Christian Institute of Public Theology)

1.	Separation from God	2.	Idolatry
3.	Immortality	4.	Injustice
5.	Wickedness	6.	Corruption
7.	Alienation	8.	Disunity
9.	Conflict	10.	Hatred
11.	Rebellion	12.	Violence
13.	Crime	14.	Violence
15.	Moral Deterioration	16.	Deception
17.	Degeneration	18.	Isolation
19.	Demoralization	20.	Uncivilized savagery
21.	Gross Ignorance	22.	Destitute
23.	Lost	24.	Destruction and Death

God has set moral and ethical standards for mankind to live by. These standards are explicitly stated and illustrated in the Bible. God's truth, commandments instructions and living standards are for the good of man. When they are violated, man's civility, welfare and life degenerate and dissipate.

SPIRITUAL ILLNESS
Dysfunctional Symptoms

1. Denies Reality
2. Negates Truth
3. Extinguishes Enlightenment
4. Defies Authority
5. Confuses Logic
6. Chooses Irrationality
7. Ignores Merit
8. Dispenses Rationality
9. Obstructs Justice
10. Obliviates Righteousness
11. Mocks Beauty
12. Demeans and rejects Love

The variations and intensities of these symptoms are driven by hatred and rebellion against the Spirit and Will of God. It is an expression of the futile attempt to create one's own selfishly and rebelliously motivated standards and values in defiance of the standards, values and true world realities created by God, The creator of the realities of existence. These spiritual dysfunctional symptoms lead to mental insanity, psychological destruction and death. Spiritual illness is a threat to society, humanity and civilization.

-The Christian Institute of Public Theology

THE DEMONIC AGENDA
Evil Obsessions Against the People of God
The Public Theologian

THEIR POSITION	THEIR PREOCCUPATIONS
1. Anti-God	(Worshippers of Idols)
2. Anti-Christ	(Haters of God's Will)
3. Anti Love	(Unbridled Hatred)
4. Anti-Truth	(Deceptive Liars)
5. Anti-Goodness	(Advocates of Evil)
6. Anti-Knowledge	(Imposition of Ignorance)
7. Anti-Justice	(Perpetrators of Evil)
8. Anti-Righteousness	(Majors in Wickedness)
9. Anti-Cross	(Hatred of Christ's Victory)
10. Anti-Liberty	(Violators of Human & Civil Rights)
11. Anti-Democracy	(Uncivil Contempt for Human Equality)
12. Anti-Life	Pathological Human Destructiveness

THE PEOPLE OF GOD CAN AND MUST DEFEAT THIS DEMONIC AGENDA BY EXTINGUISHING THE "Anti," prefixes preceding THE GOD-GIVEN VALUES WITH THE PRO-PREFIXES AFFIRMING THESE PRECIOUS GOD-GIVEN VALUES OF HUMAN SURVIVAL FOR HUMANKIND. BECOME THE DILIGENT PROLIFERS THAT GOD CREATED YOU TO BE IN THE ABUNDANT AND ETERNAL LIFE IN JESUS CHRIST!!!

The Public Theologian

THE SPIRITUAL AND CULTURAL BATTLEFIELD

The Warfare Against Survival Values

SURVIVAL VALUES		DESTRUCTIVE CHOICES
1. Goodness	VS	Evil
2. Truth	VS	Lies
3. Love	VS	Hatred
4. Justice	VS	Injustice
5. Knowledge	VS	Ignorance
6. Wisdom	VS	Foolishness
7. Understanding	VS	Confusion
8. Hope	VS	Despair
9. Faith	VS	Doubt
10. Godliness	VS	Idolatry
11. Reason	VS	Irrationality
12. Mercy	VS	Cruelty
13. Order	VS	Chaos
14. Peace	VS	War
15. Sacred	VS	Secular
16. Enlightenment	VS	Cognitive Deficiency
17. Righteousness	VS	Wrongful
18. Wholeness	VS	Divisive
19. Civility	VS	Barbarianism
20. Purity	VS	Corruption

SURVIVAL VALUES		DESTRUCTIVE CHOICES
21. Beauty	VS	Offensive
22. Charitable	VS	Self-Centered
23. Innocent	VS	Guilty
24. Positive	VS	Negativity
25. Humility	VS	Arrogance
26. Secure	VS	Endangered
27. Progressive	VS	Regressive
28. Goodwill	VS	Envious
29. Refinement	VS	Crude
30. Joyful	VS	Miserable
31. Inspiration	VS	Demoralization
32. Generosity	VS	Greed
33. Sacrificial Service	VS	Fraudulent Exploitation
34. Benevolence	VS	Malevolence
35. Altruistic	VS	Jealousy
36. Restoration	VS	Destruction
37. Elevate	VS	Denigrate
38. Freedom	VS	Bondage
39. Salvation	VS	Damnation
40. Life	VS	Death

The above enumerations of SURVIVAL VALUES and the opposite DESTRUCTIVE CHOICES can be clearly separated and distinguished. The human attitudes, values and behaviors of these survival values and destructive choices can be determined through a variety of human actions and expressions. These clear choices make possible wise and intelligent decisions. The loving God created man and woman in his image with the autonomous ability to make decisions based on God's knowledge, truth and wisdom. God created a dichotomy of opposites to avoid confusion. He created male and female. God created light and darkness, day and night. He created sweet and bitter; up and down, north and south, east and west. God enables man (woman included) to make choices between survival values and disobedient destructive choices. God provides the blueprint for human survival in the Holy Bible. He sent messengers of priests, prophets, kings and angels. The Bible is a comprehensive law book containing laws, commandments, principles with true principles, ethics and values to govern and guide mankind and the nations in all walks of life. Last of all God sent Jesus Christ as the unmistakable embodiment of all the survival values. Jesus Christ is the GREAT ULTIMATE I AM OF LIFE'S SURVIVAL AND SALVATION VALUES FOR ALL MANKIND. HISTORY HAS VALIDATED THE UNIQUE TRUTH OF JESUS CHRIST.

THE SPIRITUAL AND CULTURAL WARFARE IN AMERICA AND THE WORLD IN THIS 215T CENTURY, AD, REQUIRES AND DEMANDS THE STEADFAST ADOPTION OF THE SURVIVAL VALUES AS PROVIDED BY THE LOVING GOD AND SACRIFICIAL SON, JESUS CHRIST.

The Christian Institute of Public Theology

YOUR VALUES AND YOUR VOTE HAVE GLOBAL CONSEQUENCES

American Citizens
Enumerations of Values Clarification

1. Anti-America	Pro-America
2. Anti-American Flag	Pro-American Flag
3. Anti-Patriotic	Pro-Patriotic
4. Anti-US Constitution	Pro-US Constitution
5. Anti-Second Amendment	Pro-Second Amendment
6. Anti-Religious Liberty	Pro-Religious Liberty
7. Anti-Human Unity	Pro-Human Unity
8. Anti-Human Freedom	Pro-Human Freedom
9. Anti-Merit System	Pro-Merit Systems
10. Anti-Human Civility	Pro-Human Civility
11. Anti-Biblical Public Education	Pro-Biblical Public Education
12. Anti-Christian Public Education	Pro-Christian Public Education
13. Anti-Man and Woman Marriage	Pro-Man and Woman Marriage
14. Anti-Masculinity	Pro-Masculinity
15. Anti-Femininity	Pro-Femininity
16. Anti-Natural Order	Pro-Natural Order
17. Anti-Truth	Pro-Truth
18. Anti-Justice	Pro-Justice
19. Anti-Rationality	Pro-Rationality
20. Anti-Logical	Pro-Logical
21. Anti-Abortion	Pro-Abortion

22. Anti-LGBTQ Advocacy	Pro-LGBTQ Advocacy
23. Anti-Transgender Advocacy	Pro-Transgender Advocacy
24. Anti-Gender Neutrality	Pro-Gender Neutrality
25. Anti-Same Sex Marriage	Pro-Same Sex Marriage
26. Anti-Same Sex Adoption	Pro-Same Sex Adoption
27. Anti-CRT Education for Youth	Pro-CRT Education for Youth
28. Anti-Pornographic Youth Exposure	Pro-Porno Youth Exposure
29. Anti-Atheism	Pro-Atheism
30. Anti-Democracy	Pro-Democracy
31. Anti-Leadership Incompetence	Pro-Leadership Incompetence
32. Anti-Weaponization of Government	Pro-Weaponization of Government
33. Anti-Unsound Doctrines	Pro-Unsound Doctrines

Please study and check one of the 33 choices above for your value clarification

CIPT, Inc

HUMAN CONFLICTS AWARENESS SCALE

Foundations for Compatible Resolution
The Christian Institute of Public Theology

Assessment for Human Conflict Disparities

DISPARITIES (RATINGS)	Minimum (Low 0-1)	Medium (Mid 2-4)	High (Severe 5-6)
1. Conflict of Values			
2. Conflict of Spirits			
3. Conflict of Beliefs			
4. Conflict of Principles			
5. Conflict of Sentiments			
6. Conflict of Righteousness			
7. Conflict of Morals			
8. Conflict of Faith			
9. Conflict of Ideology			
10. Conflict of Visions			
11. Conflict of Allegiance			
12. Conflict of References			
13. Conflict of Philosophy			
14. Conflict of			

Purpose			
15. Conflict of Dreams			
16. Conflict of Culture			
17. Conflict of Loyalty			
18. Conflict of Devotion			
19. Conflict of Hope			
20. Conflict of Affection			
21. Conflict of Thoughts			
22. Conflict of Priorities			
23. Conflict of Interest			
24. Conflict of Feelings			
25. Conflict of Goals			
26. Conflict of Perception			
27. Conflict of Truth			
28. Conflict of Affection			
29. Conflict of Opinion			
30. Conflict of Identity			
31. Conflict of Goodness			

32. Conflict of Beauty		
33. Conflict of Love		

TOTAL DISPARITIES:

This Human Disparity scale can be applied to individuals, agencies, institutions and Nations. High Disparity Conflicts present a great challenge for resolution, civility, order and peace.

EDUCATION PROHIBITED BY RELIGIOUS DEFINITION
The Bible Defies Constitutional Religion Clause
The Christian Institute of Public Theology

The nebulous definitions, meanings and connotations of religion as used in the First Amendment of the United States Constitution, arbitrarily, mischaracterize the Bible as a part of the nebulous meaning of religion; and subsequently prohibit the unique, inexhaustible, educational, cultural, historical, social, legal and theological values of the Bible. The Bible is not ordinary, general or nebulous in its description. The Bible is not synonymous with religion as presumed in the First Amendment of the United States Constitution's "religion establishment clause."

The Bible Is a distinct, unique and specific historical, legal, ethical, theological composition of sixty-six specifically named books; combining the Old and New Testament Eras of Jewish History. It covers the whole spectrum of life from Genesis to Revelation in the New Testament. The Old Testament contains 39 books; five books of law; twelve books of history; five books of wisdom and poetry; five books of major prophets; and twelve books of minor prophets. The New Testament contains 27 books: four books of Gospels, one book of history, twenty-one letters, and one book of Revelation.

It must be acknowledged that the Bible is not a book of sectarianism, cultism or any ism that is less than monotheism. It is not a book of fiction or mythology or perceptual creations of the imagination. The Bible is a unique historical book that reveals and represents historically, one monotheistic God, one humanity, one Savior. It teaches exclusively of the existence of one omnipotent, omnipresent, omniscient, infinite, immortal and eternal God. The Bible teaches further that the worship of any entity or being less than God is idolatry. There is only one God with the capital G according to the Bible. The polytheistic gods with the small g are idols and are not the monotheistic God of Abraham, Isaac and Jacob. This God resurrected Jesus Christ from the dead. The Bible teaches against religious idolatry. The God of the Bible is the God of love and truth.

DEFINITIONS OF RELIGIONS:

The World Book Dictionary (1998, World Book, Inc) provides four credible definitions of religion as follows: (1) Belief in God or gods. (2) Worship of God or gods. (3) A particular system of religious belief. (4) Anything done or followed with reverence and devotion. These described academic and professional definitions of religion from the World Book Dictionary illustrate the expansive, general and broad definitions of religion. These general and nebulous definitions of religion clearly raise the question as to how can the specificity of the Bible and its criticisms of idolatry and dishonesty be considered as any part of a false and idolatrous religion. The Bible is not synonymous with God. It is not a book to be worshipped. It is not a being that worships. It is not a being that follows. The Bible is not a being that devotes or reveres. The Bible is not a religion. It is a book of history, knowledge, education, truth, God's love, historical acts and instructions for the salvation of mankind.

THE NATURE OF RELIGION MERITS SERIOUS STUDY:

The four definitions of religion by the World Book Dictionary are connected and related to personal and individual beliefs, worship, reverence preferences and devotions by individual decisions and choices from a universe of things, objects and beings. The core meaning of religion seems to reside in the personal feelings, belief systems and choices of the respective individuals or groups. Based on the limited information provided, a rational analysis must conclude that the Bible is not a religion. Contrarily, anything can be considered religious. Therefore, the government cannot be isolated from the definition and concept of religion. Based on the nebulous definition of religion, the U.S. Constitution and the American Government, itself, could be considered a religion.

The Bible, itself, proclaims that the worship of anything less than God is idolatry. Human beings adore, reverence and worship a variety of things, objects and beings. Religion appears to originate and reside in the minds, hearts, spirits, souls and will of individuals and groups as they focus on objects of devotion, reverence and worship. These objects, things or beings are not necessarily specifically limited or defined. The conglomerate complexities of religion and the associated consequences must not be taken lightly. Serious attention is Needed.

REVISITING THE RELIGION ESTABLISHMENT CLAUSE:

The Religion Establishment Clause is based on the First Amendment of the U.S. Constitution. The Religion Establishment Clause is used as the legal basis to prohibit the Bible from being taught in government public schools in America. This law is used to justify the prohibition of Bibles and use of Bibles in government agencies and other places of public accommodations; such as hotels and motels. The words, quotations and references to the Bible are often censured, discouraged and disparaged. Some candidates who are being sworn in for American public office refuse to place their hand on the Bible for the administration of the oath of office. The legal restrictions and public prohibitions against the Bible and the use and content of the Bible are being done without sufficient competent legal investigation and study. A serious revisit of this "Religion Establishment Clause" is urgently needed. In addition to reviewing the legality of the "Religion Establishment Clause," a competent social, national, political, economic, cultural, health, educational and theological impact study would be of great service to America and the world. The heterogeneous and technological complexities of the world have critically, narrowed the margins of error. This error is unaffordable.

THE READING AND LANGUAGE
OF THE FIRST AMENDMENT
OF THE U.S. CONSTITUTION:

"Congress shall make no law respecting an establishment of religion, or prohibiting the free exercise thereof, or abridging the freedom of speech, or of the press; of the right of the people peaceably to assemble, and to petition the government for a redress of grievances."

THE CONSTITUTION OF THE UNITED STATES OF AMERICA

RELATIONSHIP OF THE BIBLE TO AMERICAN LAW:

The influence of the Bible predates the 13 American Colonies that began about 1607 AD. Christian ministers and other Christians spread the teachings of the Bible throughout the Thirteen Colonies in America. The spread of the teachings of the Bible and the salvation news of Jesus Christ brought about eventually, what is called the "Great Awakening" in the American Colonies.

The great spiritual awakening resulted from a massive Christian-led movement of evangelistic teachings, revivals, conversions and dedication to freedom to live, work and worship without government restrictions and hindrance. It must be noted that Black Africans (Negro slaves) were first brought to the Colony at Jamestown, Virginia in 1619 and they were not considered as fully equal or equally human as their White counterparts. However, they became a part of this vibrant social and political movement in the new colonial world.

The culture of the Colonies became saturated with the ethical teachings, enlightening knowledge and liberating spirit of the biblical knowledge of the Bible and the soul salvation knowledge of Jesus Christ. The Colonists were inspired and motivated to build communities, churches and schools and to engage in free enterprise endeavors. This new beginning was inspired and sustained by the Christians and Bible believers. The Bible was their primary reading and teaching book. Many could not read or write, but they learned through the oral quotations of Scripture of the Bible. The Bible became a motivator to learn to read, write and get an education. Many schools were established during this colonial period.

Many African American slaves were motivated to read and get an education so that they could read the Bible. The American Negro slaves never considered the Bible a "White man's religion."

It was the influence of the Bible that initiated the Declaration of Independence in 1776; the Constitution of the United States in 1787. The Bible influenced the ratification of the Bill of Rights in 1791 and the recognition of a democratic form of government described by President Abraham Lincoln in 1863 as, "a government of the people, by the people, and for the people," and the issuance of the Emancipation Proclamation in 1863 that freed the Negro American slaves in 1863. In subsequent years the Bible influenced the Pledge of Allegiance to the U.S. Flag as "One Nation under God." and the American Motto on American currency, "In God We Trust." The influence of the Bible is embedded deeply in the American culture, education, social, economic and political institutions. The single most document that has made the greatest difference for good in America and the world, has been and is the Holy Bible. This magnificent, unfathomable and extraordinary gift to humanity must be respected, re-examined, revisited, reconsidered, reunited, reclaimed, replenished, renewed and revitalized.

Generations, civilizations and nations have been enlightened, guided, nurtured and strengthened by the knowledge, understanding, wisdom, spiritual concern and love contained in and radiating from the Bible.

EXPLORING THE BIBLICAL
AND LEGAL PARADOX:

Considering the massive enlightening and constructive influence of the Bible on the American culture and founding documents and Western Civilization as well; this paradoxical irony must be emphatically noted and explored. It is an egregious ironical paradox that the Religion Establishment Clause of the Fourteenth Amendment of the U.S. Constitution is used (paradoxically) to prohibit the Bible from being taught in the public government schools, along with disparaging attempts to build a wall of separation between the Bible and the government; cloaked as "separation of government and religion," and " separation of "Church and State," How is this rational, legitimate and reconcilable when the unique Bible has been influencing cultures, civilization and nations for civility and good for over five thousand years? Biblical knowledge and the foundation and guidance for the governing documents, the Constitution and the democracy of America are based on biblical influence. The Bible is the foundation for America's Constitution, Democracy and civilization's humanizing influence.

The disparagement, marginalization and misrepresentation of the Bible, in reference to the "Religion Establishment Clause" is based on dogmatic ignorance of the Bible's manifested significant truths and pro-life human values for over five thousand years of world history. The expansive disparagement and prohibitions against the Bible are also based on the false premises and presumptions that the Bible is a religion (undefined). The disparagement and subservient relegated status of the Bible in the American Government and general society, has and continues to cause tragic human deprivations, cultural damages, political corruption and national calamities beyond description and calculations.

APPEAL, REQUEST AND RECOMMENDATION:

IT IS HEREBY APPEALED, REQUESTED AND HEREBY RECOMMENDED BY THE DULY INCORPORATED CHRISTIAN INSTITUTE OF PUBLIC THEOLOGY OF THE STATE OF GEORGIA, USA

TO: THE PRESIDENT OF THE UNITED STATES; UNITED STATES CONGRESS; THE UNITED STATES SUPREME COURT

IT IS RESPECTFULLY REQUESTED THAT THE APPROPRIATE AGENCIES OF THE AMERICAN GOVERNMENT:

1. DEFINE THE MEANING AND ROLE OF RELIGION IN THE FIRST AMENDMENT OF THE CONSTITUTION OF THE UNITED STATES.
2. CLARIFY THE LEGAL PLACE, PUBLIC ROLE, EDUCATIONAL CLASSIFICATION, THE RELATIONSHIP OF THE GOVERNMENT TO THE BIBLE AS RELATED TO THE FIRST AMENDMENT TO THE CONSTITUTION OF THE UNITED STATES OF AMERICA.

The Christian Institute of Public Theology, Inc

Components for Holistic Human Understanding
Willie J. Webb

In a heterogeneous, culturally diverse, globalized and technological world, it is necessary to be familiar with ten primary components in order to be effective leaders and make enlightened decisions. The ten components enumerated below help individuals to overcome and get beyond sectarian, subcultural and provincialist boundaries. In order to be correct, relevant and inclusive in our thinking, we must adopt universal values, universal truths and universal standards. These universals must be undergirded by the whole Gospel for the whole person and for the whole world.

PREREQUISITES FOR HOLISTIC UNDERSTANDING

1. Personal Wellness (to be healthy mentally, physically, emotionally and spiritually).

2. Human Wholeness (to respect and cultivate resources and values to enhance the quality and sacredness of human life).

3. Civilized Security (to entrust human beings to be responsible stewards for the resources of God that protect and sustain human life).

4. National Unity (to create conditions to overcome divisiveness and Identify as a unified nation).

5. World Peace (there is one God, one people, one earth. Peace on earth, goodwill towards all people).

6. Social Chemistry (understanding of the personal and social results of heterogeneous mixtures of races, nationalities, cultures, religions, ethnicities, languages, customs, traditions, education and values).

7. Political Physics (understanding the organizational systems that govern, manage, influence, control and regulate rights and values).

8. Legal Mathematics (understanding the application of Divine Laws, natural laws and statutory laws that governs human behavior).

9. Economic Equity (understanding methodologies of production, distribution, allocations and consumption of goods and services in society).

10. Religious Ethics (understanding the validity, truthfulness, relevance, function, pluralism and varieties of religious experiences and fallacies).

The Christian Institute of Public Theology, Inc.
Rev. Willie J. Webb, Instructor

SUCCESSFUL LIVING BY
THE GOLDEN RULES

Sociologically speaking, human beings live interdependent group lives. Psychologically, human beings need to have conscious awareness of themselves, others and the world around them. Economically, human beings are in need of a livelihood support system. Politically, they need equitable rules and laws to govern their interactions and protect each individual with certain natural and God-given rights and entitlements. Theologically, human beings need validated instructions from the Creator of their being and the world regarding the purpose of their lives and the authoritative knowledge as to how to govern their lives in community and fellowship with each other.

Human beings on the planet Earth are blessed beyond measure and comprehension that they have been provided with an inexhaustible book from their Creator about the universe, the creation, mankind and the Creator Himself. That book is known as the Bible. It is a book with incomparable golden rules for living. It is a book of revelation from God that talks about God's involvement and engagement with mankind. It is the book that defines what is, and what ought to be. It is the book that reveals the will of God for mankind. It is the book that can be understood by science, art, law and theology.

It is said by scholars that every civilization has some form of Golden Rule in their respective language. The Bible is the ultimate rule book. It is foundational to all laws on the earth. The first five books of the Bible are law books. It is the book with the greatest knowledge, wisdom and understanding about the universe, about mankind, about life and existence itself. The Bible is the most widespread and universally known book on the earth. It has the greatest classical literature known to mankind. It is shameful, disgraceful, pathological and sacrilegious that such a book, such a precious invaluable gift could be so neglected and marginalized. The Bible is the book that documents the birth, life, teachings, love, crucifixion, resurrection and ascension of the Savior of the world, Jesus Christ, with invincible evidence and infallible proof. This is the individual that was born, lived, crucified, arose from the dead and ascended in history. Jesus Christ is the historical event that splits history in B.C. and AD.

GOD PRIORITIZES HUMAN LIFE
Human Life Bears the Image of God
The Christian Institute of Public Theology

HUMAN LIFE MADE IN THE IMAGE OF GOD

So, God created man in his own image, in the image of God created he him; male and female created he them. And God blessed them, and God Said unto them, be fruitful, and multiply, and replenish the earth, and subdue it: and have dominion over the fish of the sea, and over the fowl of the air, and over every living thing that moveth upon the earth. (Genesis 1:27-28).

BIBLICAL REFERENCES TO MOTHERS

James Strongs Exhaustive Biblical Concordance enumerates more than 327 references to the words mother and mothers in the Old and New Testaments of the Bible. It would be most fruitful and enlightening to study the biblical historical roles of mother and mothers in the Bible. These most significant roles and purposes of mother references are grossly neglected in the general society.

BIBLICAL REFERENCES TO WOMEN

James Strong's Exhaustive Biblical Concordance provides 539 biblical references to women in the Bible. The study of the roles and history of women in the Bible has the potential to be revolutionary in understanding the significant roles women have played in history. It is a much-needed enlightenment during this gross gender confusion in the 21st Century.

BIBLICAL REFERENCES TO THE WOMAN'S WOMB

Strong's Exhaustive Biblical Concordance provides 73 biblical references to the woman's womb in the Old and New Testaments of the Bible. A serious in-depth study of the various incidents of barren women and those who gave birth under varying circumstances in the Bible, adds new perspectives, insights and revelations. The extenuating circumstances of adultery, promiscuity, rape, sodomy, bestiality and other sexual involvements are very enlightening from the biblical perspective.

A QUOTE OF THE WOMB FROM JEREMIAH

"Before I formed thee in the belly I knew thee, and before you came forth out of the womb, I sanctified thee and ordained thee a prophet for the Nations."

(Jeremiah 1:5)

This passage provides extraordinary insight into the human life in the womb before the child is born. This highlights the significance of foundational Scriptural knowledge in regards to the significance of the fetus in the womb. The Bible provides a new perspective and a higher authority to evaluate the value and significance of unborn children.

A QUOTE OF THE WOMB FROM LUKE

"And when the eight days were accomplished for the circumcising of the child, his name was called JESUS, which was so named of the angel before he was conceived in the womb."

(Luke 2:21)

For, lo, as soon as the voice of the salutation sounded in mine ears, the babe leaped in my womb for joy."

(Luke 1:44)

GOD IS THE PRO-HUMAN LIFE GOD

"For God so loved the world that he gave his Only Begotten Son that whosoever believe in him should not perish but have everlasting life."

(John 3:16)

JESUS IS THE PRO-HUMAN LIFE SAVIOR

"The thief cometh not, but for to steal, and to kill, and to destroy I am come that they might have life and that they might have it more abundantly."

(John 10:10)

THE DECLARATION OF INDEPENDENCE IS PRO LIFE

"We hold these truths to be self-evident that all men are created equal and are endowed by their Creator with certain unalienable rights; Among these are life, liberty and the pursuit of happiness."
It is interesting that the word, "created" is used instead of the word, "born."

THE FOURTEENTH AMENDMENT OF THE U.S. CONSTITUTION IS PRO LIFE

All persons born or naturalized in the United States and subject to the jurisdiction thereof, are citizens of the United States and of the State wherein they reside. No State shall make or enforce any law which shall abridge the privileges or immunities of citizens of the United. States; nor shall any State deprive any person of life, liberty, or property, without due process of law; nor deny any person within its jurisdiction the equal protection of the laws.

THE PLEDGE OF ALLEGIANCE TO THE FLAG AND US CONSTITUTION ARE PRO LIFE THE AMERICAN MOTTO, 'IN GOD WE TRUST," IS PRO LIFE

THE EMANCIPATION PROCLAMATION IS PRO LIFE

THE UNITED STATES OF AMERICA IS EXCEPTIONALLY BLESSED TO BE A PRO LIFE NATION

THANK GOD FOR THE BOUNTIFUL BLESSINGS AND SHARE THEM ABROAD

The Christian Institute of Public Theology

INDIVIDUAL AND GROUP CHOICES OF SELF–DESTRUCTION
Warning for the Righteous and the Wicked
(Ezekiel 3:18-21)

1. Superficial Priorities
2. Mundane Preoccupation

3. Majors in Minutia
4. Indulges Foolish Absurdities
5. Squanders Time
6. Specializes in Trivia
7. Self Imposes Ignorance
8. Indulges Self-Centered Living

9. Savors Exploitive Disposition
10. Complacent About Life
11. Comfortable with Mediocrity
12. Wanders Aimlessly

13. Selectively Miseducates
14. Lives A Life of Cowardice
15. Afraid to Live, Scared to Die
16. Lacks Faith & Courage to Live
17. Refuses to Choose Abundant Life
18. Ungrateful for Precious Life
19. Preoccupied with Condemnation
20. Consumed by Selfishness

21. Addicted to Worldliness
22. Blame Others for Personal Failures
23. Chooses Darkness over Light
24. Self-Deceptive Dishonesty
25. Forfeits God's Gifts
26. Avoids Noble Thoughts
27. Rejects Godly Life Purpose
28. Refuses Salvation Faith in Jesus
29. Embraces Hopelessness
30. Indulges Unethical Values
31. Practice Immoral Behavior
32. Adheres to Dogmatic Ignorance
33. Adopts Anti Education Attitude
34. Accepts Biblical Illiteracy
35. Perpetuates Hatred Addiction
36. Rejects Jesus Christ as Lord
37. Refuses to Love God & Neighbor
38. Refuses Spiritual Awakening
39. Chooses Anti-God Existence
40. Surrenders to Death & Perdition

GOD HAS PROVIDED THE WAY OF LIGHT, TRUTH AND LIFE
THEY ARE EXPRESSED EXPLICITLY IN THE BIBLE AND JESUS CHRIST

The Dilution of Survival Values

Basic Truths:

All have sinned and come short of the glory of God.
He that is without sin, let him cast the first stone.
Judge not that you be not judged.
Be not deceived, God is not mocked,
whatsoever a man soweth that shall he also reap.
Spiritual Discernment:
"Beloved, believe not every spirit, but try the spirits,
and see if they are of God. (1 John 4:1)"

The Congruence of Truth:

True religion, true science, true art and true divine law do not
conflict with each other. The pseudo-religions, pseudo-
science, pseudo art and pseudo-laws conflict with each other.

Basic Foundational Truths:

God's Creationism as taught in the Bible is true.
God's (ID) Intelligent Design in Creation is true.
God's revelation in the Bible is true.
God's Revelation in Biblical Prophecy is True.
God's Revelation in Jesus Christ is True.

Faith in the Revelatory Truth of God:

The faith in these truths became highly concentrated in
America between 1600 and 1970. Black African Americans

expressed a greater concentration of these truths than others. These concentrated survival values blessed America to become a prosperous, powerful and blessed country due to these values of truth and faith in God.

The Concentration of Survival Values Correspond with Racial Segregation:

The Black African Americans developed the most nonviolent and civilized values known. In the midst of slavery and oppression, they built families, churches, schools and communities and businesses. No other group had ever done so much with so little and against such great odds. Their strides coward civilization, self-help and altruism bear the hallmarks of a great people. The richness of cultural, educational, social, civil and artistic achievements reached their zenith during the segregated and oppressive era in American history.

The Dilution of Survival Values

The integration and globalization beginning in the 1970s began to dilute the survival values of Black African Americans. The most significant achievements of Black Americans were by the Black Americans who were reared and socialized in a racially segregated society. The concentration of Black survival values contributed significantly to strengthening America. It is ironic that similar social forces that diluted the survival values of Black Americans are now diluting the survival values of America. America has become a borderless country with a diminishing national identity with no standards and loss of identity.

THE SEVENTH ANNUAL CONFERENCE OF THE CHRISTIAN ASSOCIATION OF PUBLIC THEOLOGIANS

October 19, 2012

The Keynote Address:
"Instituting Sacred Knowledge for Leadership in a Secular Society"
—Rev. Willie James Webb

Greetings in the name of our Lord and Savior, Jesus Christ, to the Public Theologians and ail persons in attendance at this, our Seventh Annual CAPT Conference. Thanks to our President, Rev. Melvin Ware and all persons who have worked on committees to make this Conference a reality.

The growing secularism in American society has become a great threat to our institutions, our quality of life and the survival values that have brought us as a people and as a Nation thus far in the Twenty-First Century. This destructive process of secularization is escalating at a rapid rate. It is fueled by advanced technology, social media and attacks on religion in the public square.

A secular society is antagonistic and is at war with God and true religion. A secular society attempts to ignore God and influence others to do the same. Secularistic people have developed policies and laws to get religion and anything that represents God out of public life. They want God and religion out of society. They believe that they can get along without God and religious values. The people who embrace secularism have objected to the mention of God in the Pledge of Allegiance. They have objected to crosses on the graves of soldiers in National cemeteries. They have objected to the Ten Commandments being located in court houses; They have outlawed prayers in the public schools. They have objected and filed lawsuits to prohibit the Nativity Scene of Jesus' birth on public property and in public places, they have objected to the name of Jesus in public prayers. Efforts are being made to get the inscription, "In God We Trust," off of the American currency. The trend continues.

The frightening thing about this trend of secularism is that it has a growing measurable impact. According to a religious research organization, known as PEW Research, there are more people in America for the first time in its history who do not claim any affiliation with religious organizations as the largest singular category. Protestantism has historically been the largest singular religious affiliation category in America. The no-religious category is the highest single category now. Parenthetically speaking, Black Americans have been the largest ethnic minority for over 300 years. That has changed in the 21st Century. Hispanics have surpassed the Black Americans as the largest American minority group in America.

The Americans and the American Christians as well as the other American religions were not culturally, spiritually or educationally prepared to receive over fifty million immigrants to America in the past fifty years. This large influx of other nationalities, religions, cultures and ideologies have contributed to the culture crisis in America. This blessed, powerful, but juvenile Country, was not prepared and was not taught how to receive, educate, accommodate and appropriately assimilate with the newcomers to America. The necessary adjustments to the large number of immigrants in America contributed to the inability of America and the Christians to deal effectively with the growing secularism. The American culture has been saturated with other diluting influences. This is not to suggest that the recent immigrants have brought bad things to America. Many have brought positive influences to America. My point Is -that the Americans and the Christian Americans were not prepared to assert the needed education, training, transformation and leadership for the newcomers to America.

The growing secularism in America is dangerous. It is a form of Godliness that is permeating and infiltrating the whole culture. It is infiltrating the government, laws, leaders, institutions, families, schools, healthcare, sports and entertainment. It is infiltrating social media and cyberspace. It is dumbing down the populous and indoctrinating the youth. It has begun a campaign to rewrite history. It has no respect for truth, facts, science, religion, law or arts. it is a Pandora Box of evil loosed in the world. You need to be sure that your church is teaching, preaching and practicing sound doctrine. You need to get involved with the educational system. You need to know what they are teaching your children. You need to know who is teaching your children. You must get intimately involved in the political process. You need to know the identification and the competence of the people who are representing you from the local and state level to Washington, D.C. You must keep diligent watch over your Executive, Legislative and Judicial branches of government from local to federal.

Secularism is bringing about another more omnibus danger to America. That danger is based on the fact that secularism is eroding the sacred Judeo-Christian foundation upon which America rests. The US. Constitution, The Bill of Rights, the Declaration of Independence, the Motto, "In God We Trust," the Pledge of Allegiance and democracy itself is based upon the doctrines of Judeo-Christian. This foundation has made America the most powerful and most blessed of all Nations. In spite of slavery and a civil war, it Is crystal clear that God blessed America. God blessed America with the Emancipation Proclamation and the outlawing of involuntary servitude. God blessed America with the passage of the 1964 and 196S Civil Rights Acts.

However, a serious question arises through the erosion of Judeo-Christian values. Can America survive if it is shifted from its Judeo-Christian Foundation? Blind efforts are being made to shift America from its sacred Christian foundations to an antichrist and secular foundation. That is why this Nation is in confusion, division, gloom and doom because its foundations are being shaken. However, Jesus says, "Upon this rock, I will build my Church and the gates of hell shall not prevail against it." The hope of humanity is in Jesus Christ.

It is clear that the present-day leadership is leading society away from the pathways and the values that brought us out of ignorance, bondage and darkness. The blind cannot lead the blind. When the blind keep insisting that the blind lead, the blind will bring about chaos and destruction in the Nation. Their lies, false doctrines, misrepresentations, ignorance and evil are bringing the Nation closer and closer to the brink of disaster. When we talk about secularism (the exclusion of God and religious values in society) we are referring to an evil that will bring damnation, curses and destruction to the people and the Nation.

When we advocate the institution of sacred values in the leadership of the Church, the people and the Nation, we are advocating for life and for survival. The sacred must lead the secular. The secular is on a horizontal plane, disconnected from God and disconnected from the redemptive knowledge that comes from God. This disconnects from God precipitates a meltdown of survival values. A meltdown of survival values is taking place as I speak.

In the midst of this meltdown, the prophetic voices are being silenced Where are the prophetic voices? When was the last time you heard a national prophetic voice? When was the last time you heard a serious concern from the NAACP, SCLC, CBC, CORE, SNICK, ACLU American Civil Liberties Union? In the midst of this meltdown, when was the last time you heard the voice of a college or university president? When was the last time you heard from the voices of academic scholars? When was the last time you heard a national voice from the Church?

When was the last time you heard from the prophetic voice of a church leader? We have many historical and mega-churches. We have many outstanding well-known religious organizations. In the midst of the meltdown, where are their prophetic voices? Where are the watchmen? Where are the barking dogs to warn the people of the dangers that are lurking ahead?

When was the last time you heard of any significant legislation or contribution made by your political representatives on the local, state or national level? It is so unfortunate that we usually do not hear from our public officials until they want our vote and support. It is unfortunate that most, if not all, of our public officials are not representing us. They are representing themselves and their interests, not us and our interests. Because they are not representing us, they have made us a voiceless people. We cry out, but our voices are not heard.

It is unfortunate, but too often when we vote elected officials into office, we give them a free paid vacation with no supervision from us and no accountability to us. When was the last time your political representative asked you for your opinion about the pressing problems and issues that we face in our society and government? When it comes to our elected public officials, we must insist on legislation that will force them to be accountable to us and their constituency.

It is shameful that they get a paid vacation without any accountability. Let us initiate legislation immediately to require all public officials to provide quarterly accountability written reports and quarterly opportunities to meet with them to get our input. We must stop being misrepresented and misused.

Many of our elected officials do not have the competence or the qualifications to be an effective representative. Therefore, we must raise the bar. We must raise the standards and spell out the qualifications that we desire in our public representatives. We must also provide them with a job description and duties of what needs to be done. We must not continue to go on with business as usual. We must identify the problems and respond to the crisis with specific positive recommendations. I have already taken the liberty and exercised my duty as a responsible citizen to write a Job Description for the Superintendent of the Atlanta Public Schools. I have also written guidelines and recommendations for School Principals to help them to be effective in their job.

I am encouraging each of you to tell your story. Do not wait around for someone else to tell your story. If left to others, they may distort your story. You also need to learn to tell the story of your people. And while you are learning to tell the authentic stories of yourself and your people, you must also learn to tell the story of God, as God has shared with us in the Holy Scriptures. There is salvation and redemptive enlightening knowledge in the story of the African-American slaves and their Black American off springs in America. The story is rich with sacred knowledge and survival values.

Black American history is significant American history. The slaves and their off springs helped to make America the most powerful and free country in the world. The biased news media often plays down the significant contributions of Black Americans. That is why it is important to tell individual stories and share them. I am so pleased that we have the story of Booker T. Washington, George Washington Carver, The Tuskegee Airmen, Dr. Martin Luther King, Jr., Rosa Parks and many, many others. I will give you an example of the recent history of news media bias. You recall on 911, terrorists hijacked four American Airlines planes. They had plans to decapitate the head of the American Government by suicide missions of crashing one plane into the Pentagon in Washington, crashing two planes into the two World Trade Center Towers in New York City, and the fourth plane into the Whitehouse Capitol in Washington, D. C. Three of the planes found their targets. However, the fourth plane did not hit its target at the Capitol in Washington. That plane crashed in Pennsylvania. The reason it crashed in Pennsylvania, was because a young Black American Pilot refused to give up the controls to the terrorists, this heroic story of a courageous Black American Pilot never came out in the mainstream news media. We must keep the faith. We may be denied and rejected by man. God knows and he will accept us and reward us at the proper time. Just keep the faith.

Lastly, God has set the standards. Creationism is a present reality before our very eyes and ears. The heavens declare his glory. We can see it and behold it. And yet, the secular courts Rejected Biblical Creationism and decided that the schools must teach Charles Darwin's evolutionary theory and not the facts and the truth of God's Creation that is invincibly visible before our very eyes. The courts would rather accept the secular theories and reject the sacred truth. God has provided mankind a universal Book that sets the standards for all mankind. It is the Holy Bible consisting of the Old Testament and the New Testament. it is a Book that records the progressive revelation of God in history on the planet Earth. It gives the beginning and the end. It contains God's love for man and his search for man and his sacrificial gift of his only begotten Son, Jesus Christ, for the eternal sah1ath:m of those who believe and receive the Salvation Gift.

Public theology is Biblically based in the Word of God and Theologically guided by the the love, the Light and the Spirit of God.

Willie James Webb, President and Founder
The Christian Institute of Public Theology
Atlanta, Georgia

MOREHOUSE COLLEGE GOLDEN TIGERS' 50TH YEAR REUNION

Reflections by Alumnus Willie James Webb, May 13, 2011

Fellow Morehouse Classmates of 1961:

We are certainly numbered among those who are blessed by God to be alive and able to contemplate and celebrate our class reunion after 50 years. In spite of our narrow escapes from the "fire, dungeon and sword," we are still vertically positioned on our feet, clothed, sustained and in our right mind. Thanks be to God for His countless blessings and tender mercies. Let us pause for a moment of silence in memory of those classmates who have transitioned and those who are not able to be with us at this 50th Reunion.

Thanks to Richard Hope and the 1961 Class Coordinating Committee for requesting me to share some reflections on the sojourn of this unique and special class at Morehouse College from 1957 to 1961. The significance behind the providential circumstances that caused our pathways to converge at Morehouse College may yet be determined at some future time. I believe strongly that our unique educational experiences and exposures at Morehouse College have an extraordinary significance of a magnitude that will have a benevolent impact on the world for years to come.

I must admit that when we arrived at Morehouse in the fall of 1957, I was not impressed by the physical plant of Morehouse College or the AU Center.

I had graduated as president of my senior class at Tuskegee Institute High School which was located adjacent to the campus of the renown Tuskegee University founded by Booker T. Washington in Alabama in 1881. I am certain that I had been overly influenced by Tuskegee University. However, after spending a few days on the campus of Morehouse College, the "sacred and spiritual mystique" of Morehouse convinced me that Morehouse was the college where I was supposed to be.

I was highly impressed and fascinated by the lofty goals, noble ambitions, extraordinary motivations and elevated expectations the freshman year of this 1961 Class. I had never been in the company of such a high number of young Black men who aspired so highly for academic excellence and career success. It seems that each of you were aiming for MD's, PhD's and other terminal degrees. I was excited and felt challenged to be in the midst of students who demonstrated a commitment to climb the academic ladder to the very top.

Many of the Morehouse faculty members were to me, educational gurus, They were the most accomplished and scholarly academicians anywhere in the world. They were the most informed and thoroughly prepared teachers that I could ever imagine. It seems that they were especially made and commissioned by the Higher Power to teach the men of Morehouse College.

However, the rigorous demands of this well-prepared faculty at Morehouse screened out many of our classmates into early departures and caused many others to change their majors and rethink their careers. Professors McBay, Birney, Mapp, Houston and Dansby dissuaded the medical and similar ambitions of a number of students. Professors Sam Williams and Lucius Tobin caused some students to drop out of the ministry and Morehouse as well. Many of the students had difficulty in reconciling their Sunday school lessons back home with advanced and different critical theological concepts and opinions. Overall, this 1961 Class was not guilty of "low aim" prognosticated by Dr. Mays.

I had heard about Dr. Benjamin E. Mays before I heard about Morehouse College. As a student in high school at Tuskegee Institute, I had read with great interest, Dr. Mays' articles, entitled, "My View," in the Pittsburgh Courier and the Chicago Defender. Dr. Mays was the first example that I recognized as a public theologian. However, I did not know it by that name at the time. I saw Dr. Mays as a most unusual minister of the Gospel who could write such in depth critical analyses and interpretations of social and political issues and events in the South during the racial segregation era. When I heard that he was the president of Morehouse College, it provided additional incentive for me to come to Morehouse. Because of my call to the ministry, Chaplain Wynn of Tuskegee University and my high school principal, R. W. Stone, encouraged me to go to Morehouse. It would be an interesting subject within itself to learn why each of you came to Morehouse.

While at Morehouse; I received three honors of which I am still very proud. In our junior year, I, along with Clyde James, received the Benjamin E. Mays Debating Prize. In our senior year, I was selected as the, "Most Outstanding Student in Religion." Because of this honor, I was also selected to preach the Senior Sermon to the Morehouse Student Body in the Sunday Sale Hall Chapel Service. By the tutelage of Rev. Tobin and the grace of God my sermon was well received. I want to assure you that what I am sharing with you is not just about me, but it is headed for a bigger and more inclusive about all of us.

We, the Class of 1961, received a unique educational legacy at a critical time in American and world history. In 1954, the U.S. Supreme Court ruled that segregation in the public schools was unconstitutional. In 1955 Rosa Parks refused to give up her seat to a white passenger on a city bus in Montgomery, Alabama. Her actions resulted in a bus boycott and gave rise to SCLC and the advent of Dr. Martin Luther King, Jr. as a national Civil Rights leader. On October 4, 1957, the Russians launched Sputnik, a spacecraft satellite into orbit around the earth. These were among the momentous. events that fermented and precipitated the most dramatic social and political changes ever to occur in American society. It was the time when Black Southern Americans decided to challenge nonviolently the social injustices of racial segregation and discrimination predominantly in the South.

We are the Morehouse men who were at the pivot of this turbulent transition from the engrained traditions of segregation, discrimination and fear to the daunting challenge of desegregation, social equality and hope. Many of the students in this Class participated in Civil Rights marches and sit-ins. Students in this Class, including Julian Bond, participated in the writing of the Student Civil Rights Manifesto of the Atlanta University Center. The Class of 1961 rose to the occasion to make difficult decisions, commitments and sacrifices for freedom, social justice and the unalienable rights of life, liberty and the pursuit of happiness. We were prepared for these radical changes from a long list of downtrodden people who were the offspring of slaves. They continued to work even when their strivings seemed futile. They continued to hope when hope seemed hopeless. We thank God for the long list of men and women who paved the way, such as Dr. Mays of Morehouse, Booker T. Washington of Tuskegee Institute, Roy Wilkins of the NAACP, A. Philip Randolph, Rev. William H, Borders of Wheat Street Baptist Church, Thurgood Marshall of U.S.

Supreme Court to name a few. These intellectual and spiritual giants passed on to us an invaluable educational curriculum, along with an infallible ethical value system, with faith in God designed to ensure our survival in a hostile, competitive and unjust society.

It was during the 1960s when the Negro, colored, Afro-Americans consolidated their identity as being Black Americans. The racial and national identity of Black Americans came out of the Civil Rights movement. It was the time when Black Americans embraced "blackness" as a positive terminology. Black Beauty, Black Pride and Black Power became slogans and themes in the Black Community. The concept of "Blackness" transcended color and took on connotations of racial pride, strong moral character, spiritual resilience, qualities of sacredness and dignity of human life. The negative connotations and perceptions of racial blackness were transformed and redeemed into a peculiar quality and force of the soul, rooted in the historical, spiritual, intellectual and emotional depths of a people who had been tried and tested in the hot flames of injustice and oppression and who came forth as gold.

Let me summarize briefly some synchronizations and significance of the Class of 1961. This is the class that had a public theologian, Dr. Benjamin E. Mays, as President of the College. Dr. Mays, a public theologian, mentored Dr. Martin Luther King, Jr. who became the premier public theologian. Dr. King with this Black soul power and faith in God, led the most successful nonviolent revolution in history. The 1961 Class returns to Morehouse College after 50 years and is greeted by a President who encourages ministers to become public theologians. I was completing my Master of Divinity at ITC in 2000 when Dr. Franklin was President of ITC and that is when I embraced the concept of public theology. Had I not been at ITC at this particular time, I could have very easily missed out on the concept that connected my religious education regarding the, "culture crisis," and the, "social Gospel," that Rev. Lucius Tobin taught me at Morehouse. Dr. Franklin's advocacy for the role of the public theologian helped me to make that significant connection. As a result of making that connection I have incorporated two organizations with the State of Georgia in 2002. One is the Christian Association of Public Theologians and the other one is the Christian Institute of Public Theology. Based on the concept of public theology and the two incorporated organizations, I have published a book entitled, The Way Out of Darkness: Vital Public Theology. The concepts of public theology, the two incorporated organizations and the Way Out of Darkness is what is needed at this critical time in history to resurrect, incorporate and complete the missions started by NAACP and SCLC. The success of Dr. King as a premier public theologian is the key. He embraced and practiced the concepts of public theology. Public theology has the vertical dimension up to the will of God. Our problems are too serious and dangerous now to depend on political, secular and horizontal dimensional solutions.

I have not begun to scratch the surface on the significance of the 1961 Class. This is a class that produced a president of Morehouse College in the class member of Leroy Keith. This is the class that has a son of a president of Morehouse College, Richard Hope. Had Richard not asked me to share reflections for the 1961 Class, most of this information would have been dormant. Thanks to George Grant who has made a great effort to increase. our communication and sharing. I believe that it is critical that we make every effort to share and publish our experiences that were conceived through our exposures at Morehouse College.

Morehouse men of 1961, I am proud to be one of you. Your self-actualization and personal accomplishments compel me to respect you and cherish our friendships and fellowships. Our academic challenges, intellectual debates, athletic competition, moral struggles, success and failures, joys and sorrows and our mutual companionship has been our inspiration and our propelling incentive for the future.

May God bless us and keep us and our families in his care. May God bless Morehouse College. May the Class of 1961 pass on this legacy. May the legacy of Morehouse College live forever.

In the service of our Lord,
Willie James Webb, Class of 1961
May 13, 2011, 50th Class Reunion

CHAPTER 3
BLESSINGS OF GOD

God's Will Is Made Known to Mankind

The Bible contains the Word of God and the Will of God. God's Will is revealed in God's Word. Why do so few people know the Will of God when it is not a secret? God has made his Will known to humanity. God's Will is further revealed in his creation of light, life, truth, justice, goodness, righteousness, love, peace, beauty, mercy, knowledge, wisdom and understanding. God loves humanity so much that he made known his Will, ways, truth, wisdom and understanding to those who seek, ask and knock. God personalizes his Will in Jesus Christ. Jesus Christ is not a secret. His name is exalted above every name. "For God so loved the world, that he gave his Only Begotten Son, that whosoever believeth in should not perish, but have everlasting life (John 3:16)." Jesus Christ is the undeviating Will of God to reach mankind. Jesus is the way, the truth and the life (John 14:6). It is the duty, honor, privilege and blessing for every person to find out the Will of God for the world and for one's own life. The revelation of God's Will in Jesus Christ is the best Good News for mankind. How shall we escape if we neglect so great salvation? (Hebrews2:3)

Attention All People of the Earth

In The Year of Our Lord two thousand years ago, God made a personal visit to the earth in his Only Begotten Son Jesus Christ. He came personally to be a sacrifice for our sins and to give life more abundantly and eternal life to them who believe. Yes, God came to his world on the earth in Jesus Christ. He was born in history. He lived in history. He was crucified (sacrifice) in history. He was resurrected in history. He ascended back to God in history. The Holy Bible is the Sacred Record of what God has done for mankind in history. Every man, woman and child can be saved by believing on the name of Jesus Christ, the name that is above every name. JESUS LIVES. He is the WORD that became flesh and dwelt among us according to the Gospel of St. John. Yes, he came in the flesh two thousand years ago. Some people did not recognize the time of his visitation. Some people still do not recognize that most historic visit. Don't be like them. Accept Jesus today in your heart.

The employment of spiritual power can get things done that otherwise seem impossible. The economic decline in America can be reversed through spiritual power. Crime and evil can be overcome through spiritual power. Spiritual power can be generated through fervent prayer, meditation on God's Word, faith in God and courageous actions in the name of God.

SPIRITUAL POWER

Spiritual power can be demonstrated through love, compassion for those in need, wisdom and understanding, hope, faith, goodness, righteousness and persistence by the grace of God. God is the source of spiritual power. This spiritual power is available to those who believe in God through faith. This spiritual power is available to individual persons and groups. and nations. Spiritual power is available to be used for the redemption and salvation of God's people and to the glory of God. God's empowerment through His Spirit is available for those who believe through faith.

Noah Found Favor with God

God has told humanity in the Bible about things that will happen on the earth. There are 935 references to the earth In the Bible. It talks about whirlwinds, floods, famines, droughts, pestilence, fires, earthquakes, wars and rumors of wars. Hurricane Harvey in Houston Texas in August 2017 and Hurricane Katrina in New Orleans, Aug. 2005, are reminders of what God has spoken in the Bible. Noah found favor with God. God gave him instructions to build an Ark for the saving of Noah, his family and the animal kingdom. Genesis, chapters 6-10 gives the story of how Noah found favor with God and was saved from the flood. Ungodly leaders who do not acknowledge God are dangerous to humanity. They hinder the warning, revelation, preparation and salvation provided by God. God has provided mankind with science and technology to protect human life. The ungodly man is ignoring the warning. Man can find favor with God.

The Power of Faith Engagement

There is nothing more empowering for a person than faith in God. The 11th Chapter of Hebrews contains a long list of heroes of faith and the spectacular and miraculous accomplishments by faith. Unfortunately, this faith power given by God is grossly underutilized. One reason that it is underutilized, is because it requires work. It requires doing something positive for someone or for humanity in general. The Book of James 2:26 says, "Faith without works is dead."

There is a vital need in this generation to unleash your power of faith through good works. Jesus said in Matthew 17:20 that Faith, "as a grain of mustard seed," has the power to move a mountain. Paul told the Philippians (4:13), "I can do all things through Christ which strengthens me." Unleash your power by serving humanity through faith in God. Find your purpose and fulfill your mission by the empowerment of faith. Use the windows of opportunity to use your faith. We have limited time. Jesus said, "I must work the works of him that sent me while it is day: the night cometh when no man can work."

God's Blessed Assurance

Even when your people and the world let you down and reject you, God loves you. How comforting it is to know that the Almighty God cares about you even when you are forsaken by the world. God is love. God is always available. God has all the power. God can do more for you than the whole world. In Jesus, God has sent us a Savior and a friend who is closer than a brother or sister. Jesus extends to us these comforting words: "Come unto me all ye that labor and are heavy laden and I will give you rest. Take my yoke upon you, and learn of me: for I am meek and lowly in heart: and ye shall find rest unto your souls. For my yoke is easy and my burden is light." (Matthew 11:28-30). Let not your heart be troubled: Ye believe in God, believe also in me." (John 14:1). Having been assured of God's blessings, let us go forth with new hope, renewed courage, increased faith, more love and be blessed and be a blessing to others.

THE UNIVERSAL UNIQUE BOOK OF GOD
THE HOLY BIBLE

1. THE BOOK OF MONOTHEISM
2. THE BOOK OF THE ETERNAL GOD
3. THE BOOK OF THE TRIUNE GOD
4. THE BOOK OF JESUS CHRIST
5. THE BOOK OF CREATION
6. THE BOOK OF UNIVERSALITY
7. THE BOOK OF ULTIMATE AUTHORITY
8. THE BOOK OF THE CELESTIAL AND TERRESTRIAL
9. THE BOOK OF SPIRITUALITY
10. THE BOOK OF LIGHT
11. THE BOOK OF TRUTH
12. THE BOOK OF LOVE
13. THE BOOK OF KNOWLEDGE
14. THE BOOK OF CIVILIZATION
15. THE BOOK OF GOODNESS
16. THE BOOK OF JUSTICE
17. THE BOOK OF WISDOM
18. THE BOOK OF COSMOLOGICAL ORDER
19. THE BOOK OF LAW
20. THE BOOK O.F RIGHTEOUSNESS
21. THE BOOK OF DIRECTIONS
22. THE BOOK OF ART
23. THE BOOK OF BEAUTY
24. THE BOOK OF REALITY
25. THE BOOK OF PRINCIPLES
26. THE BOOK OF LIFE
27. THE BOOK OF FREEDOM
28. THE BOOK OF HUMANITY
29. THE BOOK OF HOPE
30. THE BOOK OF FAITH
31. THE BOOK OF PEACE
32. THE BOOK OF NATIONS

33. THE BOOK OF SALVATION

THE UNIVERSAL UNIQUE BOOK OF GOD

1. THE BOOK OF HOLINESS
2. THE BOOK OF REDEMPTION
3. THE BOOK OF INSPIRATION
4. THE BOOK OF HUMAN HISTORY
5. THE BOOK OF THE HUMAN FAMILY
6. THE BOOK OF THE LAWGIVERS, JUDGES AND
   KINGS
7. THE BOOK OF ANGELS, PRIESTS AND PROPHETS
8. THE BOOK OF THE WORD THAT WAS MADE FLESH
9. THE BOOK OF THE DISCIPLES, APOSTLES &
   WITNESSES OF CHRIST
10. THE BOOK OF GOD'S WILL IN HEAVEN AND EARTH
11. THE BOOK OF THE GOSPELS
12. THE BOOK OF REVELATIONS
13. THE BOOK OF GOD'S MESSAGE TO MANKIND

THE BIBLE IS THE HUMAN, MENTAL, SPIRITUAL, EMOTIONAL, SOCIAL, CULTURAL, CIVIL, MORAL, ETHICAL DIAGNOSTIC PATHOLOGICAL IDENTITY DISORDERS MANUAL OF SIN, DISOBEDIENCE, FOOLISHNESS, IGNORANCE, HATRED, EVIL AND WICKEDNESS.

The Institute of Public Theology

God Invites You

God invites you to his Kingdom. What have you done with God's invitation? Have you cast it aside? Have you ignored it? Do you continue to make excuses? Or, have you rejected the invitation of God?

How many other invitations of the world have you accepted? If you receive an invitation from the Mayor, the Governor or the. President, would you turn it down?

Time is running out. God does not force you to come. The invitation is for your benefit. can you afford not to accept it? He has sent a written invitation in the Holy Bible and a personal invitation in his only begotten Son, Jesus Christ? How shall we escape, if we neglect so great salvation? (Hebrews 2:3)

A New Heaven and A New Earth
Revelations 21:1-7

And I saw a new heaven and a new earth: for the first heaven and the first earth were passed away and there was no more sea.

And I John saw the holy city, new Jerusalem, coming down from God out of heaven, prepared as a bride adorned for her husband.

And I heard a great voice out of heaven saying, Behold, the tabernacle of God is with men, and he. will dwell with them, and they shall be his people, and God himself shall be with them, and be their God.

And God shall wipe away all tears from their eyes; and there shall be no more death, neither. sorrow, nor crying, neither shall there be any more pain: for the former things are passed away.

And he that sat upon the throne said, Behold, I make all things new, and he said unto me, write: for these words are true and faithful.

And he said unto me, it is done. I am Alpha and Omega, the beginning and the end. I will give unto him that is athirst of the water of life freely.

> He that overcometh shall inherit all things;
> and I will be his God, and he shall be my son.

God Forgives and Heals

God wants his people to be healthy, whole and at peace with each other. However, all forms of sinfulness and sickness are raging in our world. Jesus Christ is the Great Physician. When he walked the earth, he demonstrated his ability to heal bodies, minds, spirits and souls. He resurrected some from the dead. He gave sight to the blind, hearing to the deaf and walking ability and agility to the lame. He healed persons with leprosy and those who were paralyzed. He cast out demons. He rescued a woman who was about to be stoned to death by a mob of unhealthy and misguided people. God and his Only Begotten Son Jesus Christ are still in the healing business. All individuals and nations need this healing. 2 Chronicles gives us God's requirement for forgiveness and healing: IF MY PEOPLE WHICH ARE CALLED BY MY NAME, SHALL HUMBLE THEMSELVES, AND PRAY, AND SEEK MY FACE, AND TURN FROM THEIR WICKED WAYS; THEN WILL I HEAR FROM HEAVEN, AND WILL FORGIVE THEIR SIN, AND WILL HEAL THEIR LAND (2

Chronicles 7:14). Let us begin individually to meet this requirement and pray that it spreads throughout the earth.

Christmas

Be sure to embrace the significance of Christmas this year as never before. Count your blessings and embrace them with gratitude. Embrace Christmas for yourself, your people and the world. Look beyond the worldly presents and seek the presence of Christ. The goodwill and worldly gifts can be wonderful blessings. However, we must realize that Jesus Christ is the greatest personal gift to all humanity and to the world. This is the gift that became flesh and dwelt (dwells) in our midst and in our hearts. This was and is a sacrificial gift of love and eternal life to all who will receive it. Embracing this gift can transform our lives into new creatures in Christ. After two thousand years, men, women, boys and girls are still fighting and hating on each other. There are still wars, rumors of wars, heathenism, brutality, violence, injustice, envy, jealousy and disobedience. Let us allow the Holy Spirit of Christmas to transform our lives. Study John 3:16.

Thanks Be to God

Thank God for everything. Thank God for his excellent Creation. Thank God that he saw fit to include you and me in his excellent creation. God created everything from nothing. He created you and me from nothing. God created you and me as beings who can recognize existence and see his handiwork in his marvelous creation. Why thank God? In addition to creating us from nothing with eyes, ears minds and spirits to behold his creation, God made us special. He created us in his own image and likeness. There is something about human beings that is like God. Thanks be to God. He gave us the ability to be fruitful and multiply, replenish the earth and subdue it; and to have dominion over the fish of the sea, the fowl of the air and every creature that moves upon the earth. Why thank God? God has crowned humanity with glory and honor. He has made us new creatures in his only Begotten Son. He has given us the abundant and eternal Life in Jesus Christ. God has accepted us in his Household of Faith. O' Lord, our Lord, how excellent is thy name in all the Earth!

The Gift of Human Life
(Overcome Fear and Live)

The gift of human life made in the image of God is the most sacred and precious gift of God. God has made the earth a place of habitation and support for human life. The earth is a place with resources to support, nurture and sustain human life. The protection of human life and the earth that sustains life are the utmost priorities on the planet earth. Jesus came to give life and to give life more abundantly (John 10:10). Jesus opposes everything that hurts human life. Jesus brings goodness, truth and light to overcome evil, ignorance and darkness. In order to protect this human life, Paul tells the Ephesians (6:11) to put on the whole armour of God. We must not be negligent or lackadaisical in the protection of human life. The basic goals of our laws and institutions of society must be to protect human life. Human life is so precious that God extends life after death to eternal life to be with God forever (John 3:16).

God is always with Us

It is good news to know that God is omnipresent. God is never absent from our lives. Psalm 39:7-12, declares, that no one can get away from or escape from the presence of God. God knows all about us and what we are going through and what we are experiencing. God knows all about our abuse, mistreatment, dis appointments, broken hearts, trials and tribulations. However, through it all, we are not alone. God is with us. God told Joshua, "As I was with Moses, so will I be with you." Hardships will come, especially when you are striving to do the right thing. Saint Paul endured severe hardships and suffering. He told the other apostles, "We are troubled on every side, yet not distressed; we are perplexed, but not in despair; persecuted, but not forsaken; cast down, but not destroyed." (2 Cor. 4:8-9). God has promised never to leave us nor forsake us. He promises to be with us eternally. Since we have this blessed assurance of God's presence, let us go forth; unafraid, with new determination and faith, to live courageously to fulfill our hopes and dreams and be all we can be in Jesus Christ, our Lord and Savior. CLAIM VICTORY IN CHRIST!

The Giving and Loving God

Thanks be to God for all his infinite gifts and love. Thank God for his marvelous and wonderful creation for all humanity to behold. "O Lord, our Lord, how excellent in thy name in all the earth." Thanks be to God for life, each life, every life, your life and my life. Thanks be to God for our bodies, minds and spirits. Thanks be to God for the habitation of the earth; for its food, water, clothing shelter and beauty.

Thank God for the support systems and the bountiful resources that support and sustain human life. Thank God for blessing the nations of the world and the United States of America. Thank God for the cosmological order of the universe and its intelligent and beautiful design. Thank God for true religion, divine laws, the observation and rationality of science and the harmony and congruence of art. Thanks be to God for the life giving and nurturing power of faith, hope and love. Thank God for the Only Begotten Son, Our Lord and Savior, Jesus Christ, who said, "I am come that they might have life, and that they might have it more abundantly." (John 10:10)

For God So Loved the World
(John 3:16-21)

For God so loved the world that he gave his Only begotten Son; that whosoever believeth in him should not perish, but have everlasting life.

For God sent not his Son into the world to condemn the world; but that the world through him might be saved:

He that believeth on him is not condemned: but he that believeth not is condemned already, because he hath not believed in the name of the Only begotten Son of God.

And this is the condemnation, that light is come into the world. and men loved darkness rather than light, because their deeds were evil.

For every one that doeth evil hateth the light, neither cometh to the light, lest his deeds should be reproved.

But he that doeth truth cometh to the light. That his deeds may be made manifest, that they are wrought in God.

The Matchless Love and Gifts of God

Consider the matchless gifts of God, and you will be humbled, gratified and amazed. God gives you life through your mother and father. He gives you a human family and a place to live on the earth, He gives you air to breathe, water to drink, food to eat, clothing to wear, shelter to protect and an environmental support system to sustain life. God gives you eyes to see, ears to hear, nose to smell, skin to feel, a mind and a spirit to discern and behold the majestic glorious wonders of the earth and the heavens. He gives you light and truth to direct your pathway. He gives you a self-will to choose that which is good, just and righteous. God gives you a spirit to relate to him and to your sisters and brothers. God gives you eternal life through Jesus Christ. God's giving is an expression of his infinite love for life and his omnipotent power to sustain life. God loves us so much that he gives us the capacity to witness the marvels and mysteries of existence and creation. God has made us witnesses of the bountiful earth, the hanging moon, the shining sun and the twinkling stars. How will you show your gratitude to God?

CHAPTER 4
THE GENEROSITY OF GOD

GOD'S ASTOUNDING GIFTS TO MANKIND

God's incomparable and unique gifts to mankind are the most astounding, incredible blessed conceivable revelation possible. GOD MADE MAN IN HIS OWN IMAGE. God created male and female, man and woman in his own image (Genesis 1:27). How awesome is the thought, that God made man in his image! What a glorious gift! What a special recognition! What a special and magnificent honor to be made in the image of God! God blessed the man and the woman with the ability to be fruitful, multiply, replenish the earth, subdue the earth; and have dominion over the fish of the sea, fowl of the air and over every creature that moves on the earth (Genesis 1:28). God gave man an autonomous creative mind, an agile dexterous body that stands, walk and run upright. God gave man a spiritual nature that transcends the physical and communes with man and God. God gave man dominion on the earth, a Biblical Book of Life and His ONLY BEGOTTEN SON, JESUS CHRIST, FOR MAN'S ETERNAL LIFE!!!

The Extraordinary Generosity of God

The Bible is the magnificent revelation of God's innumerable gifts to mankind. God shares with mankind the magnificent and majestic revelation of creation. God shares the excellency of his creation of the universe with mankind. He even shares his creation of the man and the woman. God made man and woman in his image and blessed them. He gave them positions of authority and dominion on the earth. God shares his progressive historical revelation from the beginning to the end with mankind in Alpha and Omega. God shares his love with mankind throughout history. God sends priests to mediate and petition. God sends kings to govern and reign. He sends prophets to watch, to warn, to proclaim, to guide and to prophesy. He sends angels with messages and mercy. He sent his Only Begotten to provide lordship, salvation, abundant and eternal life. He gives peace and joy; grace and mercy. He gives knowledge, wisdom and understanding. He gives light to see out of and through the darkness. God makes available the mind of Christ. Paul says in Philippians 2:5, "Let this mind be in you that was also in Christ Jesus." God loves mankind with an un conditional and everlasting love. Thanks be to God!

The Ways of Justice

The ways of justice are divine and eternal. Justice is a condition created by God to maintain balance in the human enterprise. It is desirable and achievable by the righteous and conscientious efforts of people of goodwill. It is the natural way. It is the way of nature and the universe. It is the logical way. Justice makes sense. It is scientific, but not limited to science. Many aspects of justice are measurable. It suggests evenness and equality. The complexities of human involvement and human behavior frequently rule out simplistic decisions. Therefore, the process of arriving at justice in many instances can be as intricate as problems in biochemistry or physics. And that is why it is mandatory, that those who are in positions to administer justice, must be capable of understanding and dealing affectively with the intricacies of legal mathematics, social chemistry and political physics.

The way of human justice is the democratic way. Its power is derived from the consent of the governed. Its final authority is from God. Justice is the constructive way. It minimizes friction, increases balance and enhances stability in the society. Justice increases cohesion and solidarity among the members of the society. Justice is the human way. It is the way of enlightened civilization. It represents cultural and social refinement. Human justice is the way of righteousness. Righteousness is the way of God. It represents the deep yearning of the human spirit for unity, peace and the brotherhood and sisterhood of all human beings.

Excerpt from Psychotrauma: The Human Injustice Crisis, pp. 100-101, Author, Willie James Webb

The Excellency of God
(Psalm 8)

O LORD our Lord, how excellent is thy name in all the earth! Who has set thy glory above the heavens.

Out of the mouth of babes and sucklings has thou ordained strength because of thines enemies that thou mighties still the enemy and the avenger.

When I consider thy heavens, the work of thy fingers, the moon and the stars, which thou has ordained;

What is man, that thou are mindful of him? And the son of man, that thou visitest him?

For thou has made him a little lower than the angels, and has crowned him with glory and honor.

Thou has made him to have dominion over the works of thy hands; thou has put all things under his feet. All sheep and oxen, yea, and the beasts of the field;

The fowl of the air, and the fish of the sea, and whatsoever passes through the paths of the seas.

O LORD our Lord, how excellent is thy name in all the earth!

Foundations for All Human Life

Christian ethical, moral and spiritual values are essential foundations for all other human values. Without true ethical, moral and spiritual values, human beings have no reliable guide or purpose driven meaning for their lives. They are existing and operating in darkness and in a world of confusion. Human beings without Godly moral and ethical values are like robots without a thinking mind; without a loving heart; without any reverence or soul connection with God. Human beings are socialized and civilized by the teaching of moral and ethical values. All human beings, including our most noble professionals, such as teachers, doctors, lawyers and preachers are dangerous to humanity without Christian ethnics and moral standards. Injustice, crime, wickedness and evil are rampant in society. God has given us the answers and solutions in abundance to eliminate crime, sin and evil. These lessons, solutions, remedies and prescriptions are written in the Bible. All other knowledge, education and values must be undergirded by the foundations of God's Word of Truth. We must get busy teaching God's Word to save ourselves.

A Season for Everything
(Ecclesiastes 3:1-8)

For everything there is a season, and a time to every purpose under the heaven: A time to be born, and a time to die; a time to plant, and a time to pluck up that which is planted;

A time to kill, and a time to heal; a time to break down, and a time to build up; A time to weep, and a time to laugh; a time to mourn, and a time to dance;

A time to cast away stones, and a time to gather stones together; a time to embrace, and a time to refrain from embracing; a time to get and a time to lose; a time to keep, and a time to cast away;

A time to rend, and a time to sew; a time to keep silence, and a time to speak;

A time to love, and a time to hate; a time of war and a time of peace.

Cultural Transformation Strategy

The American culture needs transformation. The decadent cultural meltdown must be reversed. It can be re versed. It can be reversed and transformed. The transforming power must come from above. That power from above is available to each of us to begin the cultural transformation. The strategy is found in the Word of God. The power is in the Spirit of God. The methodology is in the mind and love of Jesus Christ. Romans 12:2 provides the core Scripture for cultural transformation: "And be not conformed to this world: but be ye transformed by the renewing of your mind." Serious and sincere study of the Word of God renews the mind. Regular Bible study will renew your mind. The renewing of your mind will transform you. Your transformation can inspire the transformation of others. You have the choice to transform the world or allow the world to transform you. Which will it be?

Foundations for All Human Life

Christian ethical, moral and spiritual values are essential foundations for all other human values. Without true ethical, moral and spiritual values, human beings have no reliable guide or purpose driven meaning for their lives. They are existing and operating in darkness and in a world of confusion. Human beings without Godly moral and ethical values are like robots without a thinking mind; without a loving heart; without any reverence or soul connection with God. Human beings are socialized and civilized by the teaching of moral and ethical values. All human beings, including our most noble professionals, such as teachers, doctors, lawyers and preachers are dangerous to humanity without Christian ethnics and moral standards. Injustice, crime, wickedness and evil are rampant in society. God has given us the answers and solutions in abundance to eliminate crime, sin and evil. These lessons, solutions, remedies and prescriptions are written in the Bible. All other knowledge, education and values must be undergirded by the foundations of God's Word of Truth. We must get busy teaching God's Word to save ourselves.

God's Two Great Commandments to Man

God's two Great Commandments must direct our religious priorities. They can help us to establish what is most significant in life. God's Commandments direct our focus, concentration and guidance. God's Commandments order our minds, spirits, feet and hands. They transform our hearts into love, our speech to kindness and our intentions to goodwill and peace. God's two Great Commandments direct us to the most significant values. The most important two values are life and love. God is love. God shares his love with mankind. Without love and life, other values have no significant meaning. Jesus confirms these two Great Commandments in Matthews 22:37-39 when he says, "THOU SHALL LOVE THE LORD THY GOD WITH ALL THY HEART, AND WITH ALL THY SOUL, AND WITH ALL THY MIND THOU SHALL LOVE THY NEIGHBOR AS THYSELF." These two commandments are so basic that Jesus said that all the law and the prophets hang on them. It must be emphasized that the two Great Commandments is about loving God above and mankind below. It is not about loving material things. It is about loving life in God and loving life in mankind.

The High Cost of
Religious Liberty and Free Speech

When money and the material things of this world become your idol god, you not only lose your religious liberty and freedom of speech, your soul is also lost in the process. When a person is willing to give up his religious liberty; freedom of speech and his soul for material gain; that person has not only given in to evil, but has also joined the forces of evil. When public officials join the forces of evil, they jeopardize society, humanity and all of us. Unfortunately, there is no neutral or safe place for any of us. We are either working for evil or working against evil. Ethical neutrality, moral indifference and passive aloofness are great dangers to life, liberty and the blessings of God. First Timothy 6:10-12, gives helpful insight and instruction: "For the love of money is the root of all evil; which while some coveted after, they have erred from the faith, and pierced themselves through with many sorrows. But thou, o man of God, flee these things; and follow after righteousness, godliness, faith, love, patience, meekness. Fight the good fight of faith..."

God's Redemptive Gifts Of
Law, Art, Science and Religion

God has given us the answers and the means to solve all human problems. God has blessed man with the capacity to understand and solve all human problems through obedience to the will of God according to righteousness, justice, truth and grace. God's four distinct means for problem solving and successful living are the following: 1. LAWS to govern, control and live by. 2. ART to create, form, harmonize and beautify. 3.

SCIENCE to discover, operate, manipulate and enrich. 4. RELIGION to reform, trans form, redeem and restore. The purpose of education is to provide the knowledge, wisdom and understanding to use effectively God's gifts for remediation, restoration and continuation. Law, art, science and religion exist and operate under the jurisdiction of God. They provide the answers, means and solutions to our problems. They are undergirded and supported by the Christian faith and implemented through public theology. Public theology assures that God's gifts and other blessings are used to enhance, heal and uplift human life according to the will of God. God's gifts are for human salvation and the healing of the Nation and to the eternal Glory of God!

God's Blessing Sharing Method

The riches of God's blessings are intended for all mankind. Human justice for everyone is God's method, will, intention and plan to share the riches of his blessings. God has provided more than enough for all the people of the earth. However, many people do not get their blessings intended for them. Some people's blessings are blocked by themselves. Some people's blessings are blocked by others. Many of God's blessings are wasted and squandered by selfishness, greed, hatred and the evils of wars. However, God has instituted a system of justice. Many times, our justice systems become corrupted and fail to be Just for all the people. Justice and fairness are the way of God. Fair and just systems of merit and righteousness are being replaced by personal favoritism, arbitrary decisions and political corruption. The resulting (injustice) becomes a disruptive and destabilizing force in the society. The anti-God, anti-Christ and anti-Bible spirits are out to destroy all the rich blessings of God for humanity. The diligent learning, living and teaching the good news of the Bible will keep God's blessings flowing.

God is Ultimate Authority and Absolute Power

God is the Creator of existence and all things, including human life (Genesis 1 & 2). Every soul is subject unto God (Romans 13:1). The Bible is the ultimate written authority over all human life. God has given and commanded universal divine and natural laws to govern the universe and the affairs of mankind. Mankind does not have the authority nor the right to alter or ignore the divine and natural laws of God. God blessed his creation and declared that it was very good. God declared in the gospels of Mathew, Mark and Luke: "This is my beloved Son, in whom I am well pleased." God is pleased with the goodness of his creation, the truth of his Word and the Salvation of his Son. Therefore, when manmade laws go against the laws of God, they are invalid, unjust, confusing, chaotic and destructive laws. "God is not the author of confusion."(1 Cor. 14:33). Valid laws must be just, righteous and congruent with the divine and natural laws of God. Many manmade laws 'do not comply with the mandates of God. We must be reminded that the Bible has 192 references to fools and foolishness. Things that are not created, blessed and ordained by God's Word, do not uplift humanity, nor glorify God. The chief end of mankind is to praise and glorify God.

God is the Power and Authority

"Let every soul be subject unto the higher powers. For there Is no power but of God: the powers that be are ordained of God."

(Romans 13:1)

Every soul has a duty to be governed by the Spirit, the Will, The Power and the Authority of God expressed in the life and the sacrificial love and grace of Jesus Christ. God is undeniably over everything and everybody on the earth and in the universe. Beware of the raging heathens to exclude God.

"Whosoever therefore resisteth the power, resisteth the ordinance of God: and they that resist shall receive to themselves Damnation."

(Romans 13:2)

What must be resisted in this world today is the anti-God, anti-Christ, anti-Bible and anti-Truth spirits.

(1 John 4:1-3)

The heathens are raging. God has the Power!

(Pastor Webb)

CHAPTER 5
STANDARDS SET BY GOD

God Has Set the Standards God has set the standards for his creation and creatures. God has declared them to be good. God has set the standards for natural, physical, moral and spiritual order for cosmological congruence and balance. God has set the standards for justice, righteousness, truth, law and order. God's standards represent peace, goodness and beauty. God has provided a book with his standards for all mankind. This book of truth, love, life and salvation is known as the Holy Bible. It is the ultimate authoritative guide for all human life. No one is exempt from its jurisdiction nor the consequences of its violations. It is irrational, immoral, irresponsible and destructive to select, elect or appoint any public official or leader who do not respect and observe the God inspired standards of the Holy Bible. "Blessed is the man that walk not in the counsel of the ungodly, nor stand in the way of sinners, nor sit in the seat of the scornful (Ps 1:1).*)

The Creator, God, Owns Everything

The earth is not owned by any person, race, religious group, nationality or any designated people. Psalm 24:1 is explicit about the ownership of the earth and everything else. "THE EARTH IS THE LORD'S, AND THE FULNESS THEREOF; THE WORLD, AND THEY THAT DWELL THEREIN." (Psalm 24:1). It is a tragic sadness that there are human beings who think that they have the right or the authority to, "wipe," certain other human beings off the face of the earth or otherwise abuse, deprive and destroy them. The reprobate minds that think this way are sick with sin, in the gall of bitterness and spiritual wickedness. They are a curse to the earth and the wonderful blessings that God has created for mankind. Jesus Christ declared that he came to give life, and to give it more abundantly. The anti-Christ spirits and the anti-God spirits are determined to destroy human life and the goodness of the creation of God. The love, the resurrection, the grace and ascension of Jesus is a declaration that evil will not succeed. Every human being needs Jesus Christ as their Lord and Savior.

Keep Dreaming Alive

What are the dreams of our children? What are they hoping and living ro achieve? What kind of future do they see for themselves? There are indications that millennial children, especially in the Black community, do not dream as children did in past years. This is disappointing and detrimental. How can anyone live and look forward to the future with hope without a dream? We, the parents and the people of God must provide the educational and cultural foundations that will' cause our children to dream again. The capacity to dream is a survival value. Our hopes and dreams move us toward their fulfillment in the future. The Black African American slaves, teach great lessons on the power of dreams. They dreamed of freedom, justice and equality when these values appeared to be beyond hope. They dreamed of social justice in history and the abundant life beyond history. The slaves dreamed of a new heaven and a new earth where there would be no more tears, pains or sorrows. Let us make it a priority to create conditions so that our children can dream again.

Reflections on Labor Day USA

Labor Day is a holiday honoring working people. Oregon became the first state in the U.S. to make Labor Day a legal holiday in 1887. It is appropriate and fitting to honor working people. We must not just honor them, but we must create a just society for them to work in. Due to exploitations and other inequities against working class people, workers' rights groups and labor unions fight and advocate perpetually for fairness and justice in the work place. It is an indictment against society and the Nation that the rights and simple justice against working people are violated so frequently. This is compounded by a system of justice that does not guarantee justice at any level of appeal. This is such a serious problem, that it would be well worthwhile if Labor Day celebrations would seriously focus on human justice and fairness in the work place. Labor Day celebrations would be more worthwhile If they would focus on a judicial system that fails to administer justice. God meant for justice to be free, not something to be begged for and bought. Let us be reminded of the words of (Amos 5:24), "But let judgment run down as waters, and righteousness as a mighty stream."

The Intelligent Voter

The informed, responsible and intelligent citizen will vote for the person who reflects the sacred values of righteousness, justice, equality and freedom. Sacred values recognize the sovereignty, love and power of God. The intelligent voter will cast his/her vote for the candidate who shows evidence of being guided by the sacred values of truth, knowledge, wisdom and understanding. The intelligent voter looks for and votes for the candidate who best reflects the values that support the sacredness of human life and the best interest of society. The intelligent voter will choose by faith, the most ethical, principled, competent and honest candidate available. The intelligent voter does not vote blindly or indifferently, nor through manipulation or deception. The Intelligent voter evaluates the facts, examines the fruit, discerns and tests the spirits to see if they are of God. Ultimately, the intelligent voter will vote for the candidate who is for building the Kingdom of God instead of the city of man.

Encourage Yourself in the Lord

In the 30th Chapter of 1 Samuel, David was very distress ed because so many things had gone wrong all around him. After much grief and weeping, David encouraged himself in the Lord. David's strength became renewed in the Lord. "They that wait upon the Lord shall renew their strength; they shall mount up with wings as eagles; they shall run, and not be weary; and they shall walk and not faint." No matter what may be going on all around you, if you put your trust and faith in God, He will renew your strength. God has put source and a resource of joy within you. Encourage yourself.

Neglected Hearts and social Chaos

The American educational, religious and family institutions are neglecting the nurturing and training of the hearts and spirits of our children. The secular leaders of these institutions prohibit the teaching of character education, ethics, morals, patriotism and the Bible. The secular leaders of these institutions reject spiritual values and the reality of

God. These anti-God, anti-Bible and anti-Christ materialistic leaders are cutting off the lifeline of God to the minds, hearts and spirits of our children and others under their influence. They are blocking the door way of God. We must be alarmed and so infuriated that we will take legal action against them to open up the doorway of God for our children. The consequence of this cruel mis guided blockage of the doorway to God, is spiritual and moral deprivation that breeds mental illness, spiritual wickedness, crime, and social chaos. Social chaos is increasing because individual internal controls are being diminished by neglected hearts and spirits and the prohibition against God. Civilized societies are based on control from within the individual and not from the outside by police and dictatorial secular authority.

Responsible Citizens Must Do More than Vote

Unfit elected officials are misrepresenting their constituents and destroying democracy and America in the process. This gross misrepresentation and abuse of authority by public officials is happening because the voting citizens fail to hold them accountable. It is commonplace for public officials to ignore and disrespect their constituents once they get into office. Tragically, they misuse the public office to enrich themselves and do favors for their relatives, personal friends and associates. Too many elected and appointed public officials have become predatory exploiters of the people and corruptors of government. Greed and corruption have become so prevalent that government public policy is being set by economic bribery and administrative intimidation. Government agents are using taxpayers' money and the citizens' resources to enrich and enhance their personal ambitions. Responsible citizens have a sacred duty to clean out the unfit greedy and corrupt politicians and replace them with ethical and competent men and women who will represent the people with righteousness, justice and benevolence. We must do more than just vote. We must put ethical and quality persons in public office who believe in the sacredness of man and the sovereignty of God.

God's Requirements for Use of Power

Evil men must not be authorized or entrusted to use power. Only men (women included) with character, integrity and with reverence to all human life and to God must be entrusted to use power. Any person may do wrong. However, no person has a right to do wrong or injustice. The capability of doing wrong is not authorization or license to do wrong. God is the source of all power. God has commanded all people to do that which is right and just, love God and love neighbor as self. It is too dangerous to humanity and to civilization for evil and incompetent men to be entrusted with positions of authority and power in a technological nuclear age. Only good men and women should be authorized and entrusted to wield power and authority over other persons. Evil men and women must be prevented from positions of power. Evil men and women in positions of power must be replaced by good men and women who are authorized by God to build God's Kingdom of peace, love and goodwill on the earth for all people. "He has showed thee, 0 man, what is good, and what does the Lord require of thee, but to do justly, and to love mercy, and to walk humbly with thy God?" (Micah 6:7)

Measuring up to the image of God

How wonderful it would be to.be the person God intended you to be. God uses the seed of man, the body of woman and the breath of life as his laboratory to make every human soul in his image. God is our Father. We are his children. We were made for the purpose of God. God is the Creator. We are his creatures and creation. God is the Potter. We are the clay. "Mold and make us after thy way." In Christ, "you are no more strangers and foreigners, but fellow citizens with the saints, and of the household of God." God has given us a mind to think, the mind of Christ, a heart to love, a life to live and a soul to be saved. "We are a chosen generation, a royal priesthood, a holy nation, a peculiar people, who have been called out of darkness into his marvelous light." "Therefore, if any man be in Christ, he is a new creature: old things are passed away; behold all things are become new." In Jesus Christ, we can measure up to the image of God in us.

A Message for America and the World

Why is Jesus Christ the answer to our cultural diversity, religious pluralism and political identity politics? Jesus Christ is the answer because he transcends racism, ethnocentrism, sexism, sectarianism, regionalism, culturalism, classism, nationalism, patriotism, cultism, mysticism, legalism and humanism. True Christianity offers an atmosphere of freedom, autonomy and democracy for all people. True Christianity does not impose arbitrary standards. It allows for and encourages the optimum self-actualization of all people to live in Harmony and for the common good and to the glory of God. True Christianity is not a religion of oppression and suppression. It is a true religion of liberation, healing, restoration, forgiveness and mercy. It is an undisputable historical fact that Jesus Christ is the only one qualified to lead the awesome diversities, ethnicities and identities existing in the present technological, fragmented globalized nations and world. No other leader can claim, "I am the way, the truth and the life." "T am the light of the world." "I am the resurrection and the life." "For there is none other name under heaven given among men, whereby we must be saved (Acts 4:12)"

CHAPTER 6
DUTIES OF GOD'S PEOPLE

A Duty to Watch and Warn the Wicked
Ezekiel 3:17-19

Son of man, I have made thee a watchman unto the house of Israel; therefore, hear the word at my mouth, and give them warning from me.

When I say unto the wicked, thou shall surely die; and thou give him not warning, nor speak to warn the wicked from his wicked way, to save his life; the same wicked man shall die in his iniquity; but his blood will I require at thine hand.

Yet if thou warn the wicked, and he turn not from his wickedness, nor from his wicked way, he shall die in his iniquity; but thou has delivered thy soul.

Pass On the Blessings of God

The Creator and loving God has bountifully blessed humanity. The duty of those who are blessed is to pass on the blessing to others. Someone has said, "Give the world the best that you have, and the best will come back to you." Your blessings are better secured when you share and give them away to others. When you share and give your blessings from God to others, they will not perish, but continue to bless. It is much more difficult for thieves to steal your blessings when you have shared them with others. It is our duty to develop our God given potentials and talents and transform them into blessings that we can share with others and the world. When you share your knowledge, resources, love, services and yourself with others, you are passing on the Blessings of God. The more love you give to others the more love you have for yourself. Love is not diminished by sharing with others. There is a song that says, "You Can't Beat God Giving. The More You Give, The More You Live, So Keep on Giving." Continue passing the blessing.

HONORABLE ROLES OF MEN AND WOMEN
God's Commandment to the First Man and Woman (Genesis 1:28)

It is significant that God commanded the first man and the first woman, jointly; to be the progenitors of humanity. This commandment came from God - nor from government or any supreme court or agency of mankind. This commandment from God in Genesis (1:28) was given before Moses and the Ten Commandments in Exodus. God's commandment to the first man and woman is still in force as divine and natural laws today. God did not give this law to any government or ruler because there were none. God gave this law directly to the man and the woman. God blessed them and said unto them, "Be fruitful, and multiply, and replenish the earth, and subdue it: and have dominion over the fish of the sea, and over the fowl of the air, and over every living thing that moves upon the earth." God's universal law to all men and women; boys and girls, ought to be studied and adhered to by all humanity. By following this law, God's kingdom can be realized on the earth. Deviations, perversions and violations of God's divine and natural laws create confusion, disobedience and rebellion against God. Disobedience to God leads to destruction. Obedience to God's orders to the first man and woman will lift humanity, honor Jesus Christ and glorify God!

When Men Unite as Brothers

When men unite as brothers under the Fatherhood of God; no problem is too difficult to solve; no goal is too challenging to reach; no foe is too formidable to defeat. When men unite as brothers, the future for humanity is brighter; the burdens and hardships of the people are lighter. When men unite as brothers, friends and allies are multiplied; the power, influence and hatred of the enemies subside. When men unite as brothers, women have companions, partners, mates and friends; Children have fathers, role models, heroes, protectors and a chance to win. When men unite as brothers, families are prosperous, proud, harmonious and fulfilled; these blessings are accomplished because they line up with God's Will. When men unite as brothers under the Fatherhood of God, humanity can become one family; nations can stop studying warfare; the wicked will cease from their troubling, the weary will be at rest; no more pain, no more tears, no more sorrows. Unite men! LET THERE BE PEACE ON EARTH AND GOOD WILL TO MANKIND.

Honor to All Women and Mothers

Let us resolve to use this Mothers' Day Celebration to honor, support and promote the sacredness of woman hood and motherhood. When we honor and support womanhood and motherhood, we are honoring and supporting the human race and the Household of God. God took woman (Eve), out of the side of man (Adam), and created one flesh of the twain.

However, God chose the woman to bear all children, the boys and the girls for all succeeding generations. When men play their God given roles seriously, of supporting, protecting, respecting, loving, honoring and praising women, we are a much stronger, healthier, happier and purpose driven people by the Will of God. let us resolve this day to lift up and esteem womanhood and motherhood to the high, lofty and sacred place where they belong next to God. We must teach these lessons to our children in the home at school or wherever they may be.

The Noble Roles of Women

The roles of women, as with men, have been set by God. The roles of men and women are complementary and joint roles. They are mutually supportive roles. They are not competitive or conflicting roles. God gave a joint commandment to the man and the woman in Genesis 1:28: BE FRUITFUL, AND MULTIPLY, AND REPLENISH THE EARTH, AND SUBDUE IT: AND HAVE DOMINION OVER THE FISH OF THE SEA, AND OVER THE FOWL OF THE AIR, AND OVER EVERY LIVING THING THAT MOVES UPON THE EARTH. This commandment suggests that men and women are instructed to work in partnership, companionship and fellowship to accomplish the mission and goals set by God. God blessed and crowned woman with the exclusive role of birthing and nurturing all children. The motherhood of women is a special sacred blessing and laboratory of God to create human beings in the form of boys and girls. It is through the mothering capacity of the woman that makes it possible for a child to be born into the world. Mothers' Day is a special day to honor all women and the nobility of motherhood. Mothers, daughters, sisters, aunts, nieces, we honor you today, and every day.

Fatherhood Is a Sacred Role

Fatherhood is an honorable, sacred and responsible role assigned by God. Traditionally, fathers have been known to be protectors, providers and producers. If the family is to ever be strong again and if children are to have sufficient role models that represent strength, responsibility and discipline, Fathers must reassert the traditional role that God has given them. Fathers must teach by examples for their children to be strong, courageous, brave and true. The fathers must teach wisdom and obedience, kindness and compassion with rough minds and tender hearts. The sacredness and significance of fatherhood is reinforced as Jesus addresses God as Our Father which art in heaven, hallowed be thy Name, thy Kingdom come. This significance is further reinforced when God says, this is my beloved Son, in whom I am well pleased.

Happy Fathers' Day Men
Happy Men's Day Fathers

It is challenging to be men and fathers in a society that attacks and deprives manhood and fatherhood, beginning with babyhood and boyhood. That must change!
BOYS, MEN, FATHERS AND BROTHERS, WE ALL HAVE A HEAVENLY FATHER IN GOD. God wants you to put on the whole armour of God and stand and withstand and be strong in the Lord.

(Ephesians 6:10-18)

God wants you to, *"endure hardness as a good soldier."*

(2 Tim 2:3-4)

"Lift up your eyes unto the hills from whence cometh your help"

(Psalm 121)

"Arise, shine; for thy light is come, and the glory of the Lord is risen upon thee."

(Isaiah 60.1)

Let us begin anew this day to be the men and fathers and Brothers that God has ordained us to be.

(Pastor Webb)

The Way Out of Darkness
(Theological Responsibility, page 157)

The biblical mandates for the theological responsibility for public policy and public actions are overwhelming. From the Book of Genesis through the Book of Revelation, God is calling the public theologians to be witnesses, watchmen, stewards, disciples, educators, liberators, healers, writers, counselors, guardians, evangelists, revivalists, preachers, priests, prophets, caretakers, human service providers, visionaries, mentors, reformers, trainers, and leaders. God is calling the public theologians, the public disciples, the believers in Christ. God is calling with urgency for you to respond before it is too late! What is hindering you from your calling? What is preventing you from fulfilling your sacred responsibility? Have you conformed to the world to the extent that you cannot hear your calling? Have you been so transformed by the world that you have lost your will and courage to rise to the heavenly calling and the high calling of God in Jesus Christ?

Renew Your Mind and Be Transformed

And be not conformed to this world: but be ye transformed by the renewing of your mind, that ye may prove what is that good, acceptable, and perfect will of God.

(Romans 12:2)

Let each of us take seriously, the transformation of God's Power by the continuous renewing of our mind. A transformed people by God is needed to transform the world that is being destroyed by secularized conformity. Our transformation can transform others and the world. So, let us begin to renew our minds by seriously studying the Word of God, being obedient to the Will of God in Jesus Christ. Let people see Christ, hear Christ, feel Christ and sense Christ in you let your light in Christ shine, illuminate and radiate the Eternal spiritual values of love, goodness, truth, beauty, peace, Justice, mercy and goodwill. When you do these things, you and the world are being transformed.

Utilizing Opportunities For Personal and Spiritual Growth

God has given us talents, other gifts and potentials for growth and development. Let us fully utilize our talents to facilitate our personal and spiritual growth. Let us not cheat ourselves by forfeiting opportunities to grow and develop. God wants us to be the best we can be in Jesus Christ. When you use the talents, God has given to you, you elevate yourself and others around you. Use your talents to sing, teach, witness, praise, preach, work and serve God. God wants his children to grow up and be intelligent and mature men and women of God. Grow so you can glow so that the world can see your light shining so people can come out of darkness. Grow and develop so that you can lead the lost sheep that have no shepherd. BE ALL YOU CAN BE IN CHRIST.

Give of Your Best to The Master

Somehow, when you give your best to the Master, you are doing the very best thing for yourself and your soul. When you give of your best to the Master, you are also giving of your best to others. Giving less than the best is not good enough for God. Giving less than your best is not good enough for yourself. When we give less than our best, we not only cheat God, but we also cheat ourselves by being cheap with God. God gave to us his best in Bethlehem and on Calvary. He gave his only Begotten Son. You can't beat God giving. The more you give, the more you live. When you give God your best, as Jesus did, you will increase in wisdom and stature and in favor with God and man. (Luke 2:52). Also, Paul says that you will receive a Crown of Righteousness. If we seek God's Kingdom first and give our best to God, all other values in our lives will find their rightful place. Start this day of giving of your best to the Master and the best will come back to you.

Crisis in American Leadership

But when he saw the multitudes, he was moved with compassion on them, because they fainted, and were scattered abroad, as sheep having no shepherd.

(Matthew 9:36)

Woe be unto the pastors that destroy and scatter the sheep of my pasture I Saith the Lord.

(Jeremiah 23:1)

You have scattered my flock, and driven them away, and have not visited them: behold, I will visit upon you the evil of your doings, saith the Lord.

(Jeremiah 23:2)

Woe be the shepherds of Israel that do feed themselves! Should not the shepherds feed the flock!

(Ezekiel 34:2)

As for my people, children are their oppressors, and women rule over them. O my people, they which lead thee cause thee to err, and destroy the way of thy paths.

(Isaiah 3:12)

The diseased have you not strengthened, neither have you heal ed that which was sick, neither have you bound up that which was broken, neither have you brought again that which was driven away, neither have you sought that which was lost; but with force and with cruelty have you ruled them.

(Ezekiel 34:4)

Therefore, said he unto them, the harvest truly is great, but the labourers are few: Pray ye therefore the Lord of the harvest, that he would, send forth labourers into his harvest.

(Luke 10:2)

Wakeup Church! Wakeup America!

If we are to be saved from damnation and lamentations, we must turn from our violations arid abominations and accept the salvation of God in Jesus Christ. The people and the societies who reject the Word, the Way, the Truth, the Wisdom, the Standards and the Grace of God in Jesus Christ create iniquity, confusion, wars and self-destruction.

The parents, the schools, institutions of learning, the Church and the Nation itself must get seriously and reverently in volved in TRAINING UP CHILDREN IN THE WAY THEY SHOULD GO. Otherwise, the evil forces will teach them to hate and to destroy life, the Nation and civilization. Twenty-year-old Adam Lanza of Newtown, Connecticut is a case in point. On Friday (12-14-12), Adam Lanza killed 20 elementary school children, seven adults and himself. The HELP and the HOPE are in JESUS CHRIST!

WAKE UP PEOPLE! WAKE UP CHURCH! WAKE UP
AMERICA!

Let Us, Under God, Save America!

Let us be mindful of the significance of this special American history. This significant history of the Negro in America has salvation and survival values for America and the world. This history is significant because the love and the mercy of God worked in this history to save a helpless, despised, down trodden enslaved people from destruction. As we examine this Black and White history in America from 1619 to this 21st Century, 2014, we know that we came by faith in God. We know that it was God who led us through this nightmare to the light of day. In those days of bondage, Black Americans were in serious trouble. However, in 2014, America is in serious trouble. God saved Black Americans. Now, the Black Americans must take the lead to save America. The same values and the same God that saved Black Americans, can save America. Let us abstract the salvation and survival values from the Black American experience with God and save America. God has taught us great lessons on how to live and survive. Let teach the Nation.

Sing O' Christians, Lift Up Your Voice and Sing!

We have a Savior to sing about. Let us sing about a child is born. Let us sing about a son is given. Let us sing about the Holy Night. Let us sing about the Star of Bethlehem.

Let us sing about Mary and Joseph, the Angels, Shepherds, Wise Men and the Heavenly Father, The Prince of Peace.

Let us sing about the Word that became flesh and dwelt among us. Let us sing about the people who sat in darkness saw a great light. Let us sing about the Light of The World.

Let us sing about the man who walked on the water, and told the raging sea, "Peace, be still." Let us sing about the Man who healed the sick, unstopped deaf ears, raised the dead and gave sight to the blind.

Let us sing about Jesus who endured the Cross and was victorious over death and the grave. Let us sing about Jesus, the Way, the Truth and the Life. Let us sing about his grace that gives us Eternal life!

Sing O' Christians, lift up your voice and sing. Sing about Jesus, who is our Lord and King!

Blessed Is the Man Psalm 1:1-6

Blessed is the man that walketh not in the counsel of the ungodly, nor standeth in the way of sinners, nor sitteth in the seat of the scornful.

But his delight is in the law of the Lord; and in his law doth he meditates day and night.

And he shall be like a tree planted by the rivers of waters, that bringeth forth his fruit in his season; his leaf also shall not wither; and whatsoever he doeth shall prosper.

The ungodly are not so: but are like the chaff which the wind driveth away.

Therefore, the ungodly shall not stand in the judgment, nor sinners in the congregation of the righteous. For the Lord knoweth the way of the righteous, but the way of the ungodly shall perish.

The Transforming Journey Through the Bible

An invitation is extended to every person to take Route Sixty-Six and take a mental, spiritual and emotional journey through the Holy Bible from Genesis through Revelation. A serious, studious and faithful journey through the Bible can transform your life into a new creation in Christ. For those who love truth and the Word of God, the journey through the Bible will be the most fascinating, exciting, rewarding and transforming experience of your life. Each of the sixty-six books of the Bible is an insightful spiritual journey. Those who do not take this biblical journey will have missed out on God's Personal Love Letter of Revelation to them. They will have missed out on God's connection with mankind in history over a five-thousand-year period. Many people embark upon the physical geographical journeys throughout America and other countries. They take ocean cruises, historical sightseeing, recreational resorts, beaches, carnivals and play land activities. These physical geographical journeys and recreational excursions can be refreshing and rewarding. However, we must take special care not to neglect our souls. The journey through the Bible is a journey for the soul and the abundant eternal life, it is a journey that teaches how to connect with God. ROUTE 66 WILL TAKE YOU TO THE WAY, TRUTH AND THE LIFE! LET US INCREASE OUR BIBLE JOURNEY GROUPS!

When Men Unite as Brothers

When men unite as brothers under the Fatherhood of God; no problem is too difficult to solve; no goal is too challenging to reach; no foe is too formidable to defeat. When men unite as brothers, the future for humanity is brighter; the burdens and hardships of the people are lighter. When men unite as brothers, friends and allies are multiplied; the power, influence and hatred of the enemies subside. When men unite as brothers, women have companions, partners, mates and friends. Children have fathers, role models, heroes, protectors and a chance to win. When men unite as brothers, families are prosperous, proud, harmonious and fulfilled; the blessings are accomplished because they line up with God's Will. When men unite as brothers under the Fatherhood of God, humanity can become one family; nations can stop studying warfare; the wicked will cease from their troubling, the weary will be at rest; no more pain, no more tears, no more sorrows. Unite men! LET THERE BE PEACE ON EARTH AND GOODWILL TO MANKIND.

CHAPTER 7
BLACK AMERICAN
SALVATION VALUES

God's Grace Saved the Black Americans by the grace of God Black Americans survived 250 years of slavery, another hundred years of racial segregation and discrimination. Additionally, Black Americans are surviving fifty years of discrimination and alienation since the death of Dr. Martin Luther King, Jr. We have come this far by faith in God. In spite of all of the hardships and suffering, the Black Americans have been the most loyal Americans and the least appreciated. We have fought and died in all of America's wars. We have given our blood, sweat, tears and lives. We helped to build the most powerful and blessed country on earth, America. Our continuing presence and perseverance indicate that God has seen our tears, known our sorrows and hears our prayers. This four-hundred-year story of the survival values of the Negro in America, has a significant message for America and the world. The same God that is saving the oppressed Black Americans can save America. BELIEVE ON THE LORD AND SAVIOR JESUS CHRIST AND PUT YOUR TRUST IN GOD.

Black American History
(February, 2013)

Let us recognize with pride and humility and celebrate with faith, hope and love, Black American History Month. Black American history is among the most significant history on the planet earth. It is significant because there is evidence that

God intervened in this history to save an enslaved people whom he world forgot and looked down upon. What is significant about these people is that God did not march them across a Red Sea to freedom. God freed hem in the midst of their slaveholders. These people, not only survived, but competed and made significant contributions to the world. Black history has a message for the world. Black American history is rich with salvation messages. r is rich in art, science and religion. Let us be diligent in learning about Black American history and its heroes and sheroes, let us study Black American history along with other history and Biblical history by faith.

Black American Heroes of Faith

Our heroes of faith continue to inspire us and invite us to join the fight for social justice and freedom. The long list of Christian heroes lets us know that we are not alone on this journey for human rights, dignity and integrity. In Chapter 11 of Hebrews, Paul names a long list of heroes who did outstanding and miraculous acts by faith. There has also been a cloud of witnesses outside of the Bible who continue to carry humanity forward by faith. To name a few: Richard Allen, Adam Clayton Powell, Sr., Howard Thurman, Walter White, Mary Mcleod Bethune, Thur-Good Marshall, Booker T. Washington, W.E.B. Dubois, Carter G. Woodson, Mordecai Johnson, Benjamin E. Mays, George Washington Carver, Mahalia Jackson, Rosa Parks, Martin Luther King, Jr., Marian Anderson; Joe Louis, Jack Johnson, Paul Robeson. The list goes on and on. There are countless numbers who did not make a written list, but they made significant contributions. God has their names in the Book of Life. Heroes of faith, righteous leaders, public servants and prophetic voices are still need ed to build God's Kingdom of Righteousness.

Capturing the Spirit of Negro History

As we recapture and incorporate the God inspired Negro History in America, we enlighten and empower ourselves and America. Negro History in America has great lessons for productive living and survival values. All Americans and other people of the world would receive great benefits by studying Black American History. The study of the Negro Spirituals, The Negro Church, the Negro writings and inventions have Great enriching benefits for humanity. The study of the Black American Heroes, such as Booker T. Washington and Martin Luther King, Jr. has the potential to make a significant Positive difference in our culture and the world. It is quite evident that Negro (Black) American History is universally significant because God worked in this history to save People that the world abandoned and forgot about. The Negro American story is about a People who survived by their soul power and faith in God.

Booker T. Washington
1856-1915

Booker T. Washington is the author of his book, UP FROM SLAVERY. This is a very inspiring book. He tells his story about being born a slave and his Struggles to get an education and to educate others, Especially, the Negro race. He finished Hampton in Virginia and later founded Tuskegee Institute in Tuskegee, Alabama in 1881. Booker T. Washington had an insatiable hunger for knowledge and education. He Had a passion for removing the veil of ignorance from The Negro race. He taught the significance of educating the head, the hands and the heart and putting dignity into common labor. If a former slave can build a college and deliver the most renown speech in the 19th century, what is hindering us in this 21st Century? The reading Of UP FROM SLAVERY is highly recommended.

Cast Down Your Buckets Where You Are

The cyber space world of online technology can disconnect us from the real world and community where we live. It is becoming common place to see people so preoccupied with their cell phones and computers that they lose sight and awareness of their immediate surroundings.

There are so many online mail orders that local stores are going out of business. The walk into the store shoppers is decreasing. If you want to keep your stores in your neighborhood, you may want to consider walking in personally to shop instead of online orders from remote places. The growing preoccupation with technology threatens our personal relationship with each other, our communities and with God. The two Great Commandments require that we love God with all our heart and strength and love our neighbor as ourselves. Let us be careful not to neglect to live consciously and purposefully where we are. Let us contribute to the resourcefulness and enrichment of our communities. Booker T. Washington urges everyone to, "Cast down your bucket where you are." We are surrounded with blessings and opportunities to love and serve each other and be saved by God.

Lessons From Booker T. Washington

Booker T. Washington was a positive and constructive Builder. He did not waste his time criticizing, complaining and condemning the problems and injustices in the racial segregated society. He also did not condone them. He spent his time, energy and resources building anchor institutions and people. He worked to build and to heal to overcome the sickness, the ignorance and the evils in the American society. In addition to founding Tuskegee in 1881, he also erected over 4500 grade schools in 15 southern states through the Rosenwald Foundation. Booker T. Washington emphasized education and training of the HEAD, the HANDS and the HEART and the maintenance of HEALTH. Many schools adopted 4H-Clubs based on the educational philosophy of Washington. Booker T. Washington taught a Sunday School class at Greenwood Baptist Church in Tuskegee. He also taught a Bible class each Sun day at 3:00 pm in the Tuskegee Institute Chapel on campus. Everyone is encouraged to read his book, "Up From Slavery."

(Foundation: Educating the people of God)
Black American Heroes

Dr. Benjamin Elijah Mays was a great educator, Lead er and writer. He was the President of Morehouse College for 27 years. He hired Dr. Abraham L, Davis who taught political science at Morehouse for over 40 years. Dr. Mays was a mentor of Dr. Martin L. King, Jr. He was also the eulogist of Dr. King upon his assassination in 1968. Dr. Mays wrote a number of books. He wrote articles on Civil Rights for many newspapers for many years. Most of his articles were entitled,

"My View." Dr. Mays was a theologian and Minister of the Gospel. He required all of the Morehouse students to attend daily chapel service at Morehouse College. Morehouse College and the Morehouse School of Religion had joint chapel services before the Morehouse School of Religion joined the ITC Consortium. Upon his retirement from Morehouse, Dr. Mays became the President of the Atlanta Board of Education. Dr. Benjamin E. Mays believed in educational excellence. He believed strongly in religion, education, art and law. Dr. Mays is a great Black American Hero.

The Educational Genius of Dr. Benjamin Elijah Mays
(1895-1984)

Dr. Benjamin E. Mays was an outstanding writer, orator and educator. He was president of Morehouse College from 1940 to 1967. His educational genius was found in his ability to inspire, motivate and transform the lives of students and faculty and especially Black men. He stressed academic excellence and proficiency in the liberal arts, science, art, jurisprudence and theology. He created a teaching and learning environment that was undergirded with Christian education and values. It must be acknowledged that Dr. Mays was a Baptist preacher of the Gospel. He required all of the Morehouse students to attend daily chapel services. Each Morehouse student was assigned to a designated seat with a number in the Sale Hall Chapel. An empty seat would get the respective student a demerit. Through the educational genius of Dr. Mays, Morehouse College gave birth to two other significant educational institutions, the Morehouse School of religion at ITC and the Morehouse School of

Medicine across the street from Spelman College. Dr. Mays was the mentor and eulogist of Dr. M. L. King, Jr. Dr. Mays' advice to Morehouse students: "Be intellectually competent, morally solid and possess a genius in getting along with people."

Dr. King's Courageous, Moral Leadership

Dr. Martin Luther King, Jr. sacrificed his life to promote justice, freedom and social equality in America. His primary method was nonviolent public protests against racial discrimination and racial segregation in public accommodations. His public career began in 1955 in Montgomery, Ala. and ended in Memphis, Tenn. on April 4, 1968, where he had joined the fight to secure better wages and working conditions for the garbage collectors in Memphis. During this 13-year career the world was his platform. Universal brotherhood, equality and social justice were his themes. He gave his famous, "I have a Dream," speech on August 28, 1963, to hundreds of thousands of people. He was awarded the Nobel Peace Prize in 1964. At the time of his death, his estate was appraised at less than $5,000.00. The Atlanta Journal Constitution stated a few days ago that over half of the Congressional Representatives in Washington, D. C. are millionaires. It is quite obvious that the public officials in Washington, in the three branches of government are working for themselves and not for America or the People. Dr. King, who never served in public office, advanced America and world peace more than all the government public officials in Washington combined. Thank you, Dr. King.

Black American Children Need Your Support For Public Education

Quality education for Black American children is seriously jeopardized. Black educational leadership is incompetent, politicized and misguided in most cases. The Black educational leaders have no moral compass, ethical standards or Godly convictions. They are participating in the Godless secularization of education. They are eliminating and denying the ethical, moral and spiritual values that are essential for Black Americans to survive in a hostile and racially discriminatory society. Black Americans have survived in America only because of their faith in the merciful God of Jesus Christ. These Black educational leaders are complicit with the larger educational system, that perpetuates harassment, intimidations, demoralization and the violation of conscientious Black teachers. The neglect of children and the violation of teachers translate into the damage and destruction of public education. We cannot afford additional damage and destruction to public education. Black quality education is not only critical for Black people; it is critical for the Nation. The 400 year Black American and educational experience in America embody some of the most sacred and human survival values Known to mankind. America needs these values for its survival. Black survival is rooted in the Black Church@Christian faith.

Urgent Need for Black Deprived Youth:
Accelerated Compensatory Education

Human beings have a human right to knowledge and education to sustain life and a livelihood to keep them from perishing. A large number of Black youths are being deprived of a quality education. Many of them are depriving themselves. Many of these youth are being inadequately educated. The deprivation of education and the means of making a livelihood is genocide. A quality education, along with the technological tools for work and a just opportunity for employment are essential for a sustainable livelihood and life, itself. The high rate of school suspensions, dropouts, educational failures, lack of economic opportunities, lack of moral and spiritual guidance, are destroying our youth and our future. Educational institutions must immediately make accelerated compensatory quality education a top priority for God's children and citizens of America. Compensatory involves the necessary supports, additional personnel and services to concentrate and speedup the educational process for the students who are deprived and behind. The deprivation of a quality education is equivalent to the deprivation of life, itself. This urgent educational need must be considered an emergency requiring immediate attention!

God Inspired and Soul Expressed Black African American Music

The Black Americans have excelled in God inspired and soul expressed music in America for four hundred years. This Black soulful music covers the full range of human emotions. It expresses sorrows, disappointments, hope, faith, courage, love and the crescendo of happiness and joy. This fine art of music has been a special gift of God. It is permeated with biblical messages of redemption, therapeutic hope and ultimate salvation. Black American music has played a most significant role in the survival of the Black Americans and the enrichment of the culture of America and the world. The sacred Negro spirituals and gospel music are closely allied with Scripture. They convey great and enlightening messages about the oppressive sorrows of human beings victimized and trapped in a social environment of degradation and social injustice. The secular music of the blues, jazz and other Black music were means of using the art of music to cope with hardships and heartaches. This Black music had a positive transforming effect in America and the world. The sounds of Black music invaded spaces, places, minds and hearts where Black bodies were forbidden. We have a duty to resurrect this great musical gift of God.

CHAPTER 8
THE VITAL PRIORITY OF EDUCATION

The Urgent Priority of Education

Success in education is a top priority for every child and person. The failure to get a quality education translates into the destruction of human life. The failure of adequate education creates hopelessness and despair. Human potentials are wasted. Dreams are unborn. Investment in the future is negated. Talents and gifts of the human potential are unrealized. Humanity and civilization cannot afford this colossal failure of educational achievement. A special effort is urgently needed to make quality education a top priority for every child and person. A quality education will equip students with the essential knowledge and skills to make a positive and productive livelihood and life. A quality education will bring about: (1) HUMANE CHARACTER FORMATION, (2) HUMAN NATURE CULTIVATION, (3) TRUTH REALIZATION, (4) SPIRITUAL AWAKENING, (5) SELF ACTUALIZATION. These vital educational achievements will enable the student to find his or her best self-identity, divine purpose in life and right relationship with mankind and God. This QUALITY EDUCATION will add to the Word: GLORY TO GOD IN THE HIGHEST, ON EARTH PEACE, GOOD WILL TOWARD MEN. (Luke:2:4)

Public Education Must be Preserved

The American public education system is designed to serve the public good of society. It is an investment by primarily, the American taxpayers to educate children to be intelligently informed, productive and law-abiding citizens for the good of self and the society. Public education is designed to teach children foundational knowledge and skills to earn an honest and decent living; and to live in peace and security with other citizens and the general society. Public education is designed to provide, not just literacy in reading, writing, arithmetic and language proficiency, but also to instill good moral and ethical standards; along with social, economic and political values compatible with philosophical democratic governance and the will of God. The American public education system, along with the U.S. Constitution, were founded upon Judeo-Christian philosophy and values. Why not preserve an educational system that has served America and especially, Black America, so well?

Education: A Critical War Zone

Why go into the public education teaching field? It is a war zone. It is administration by intimidation. The classroom is often hostile, Indifferent and even abusive. Teachers are not appreciated or supported as they deserve to be. Teacher creativity and innovation are being stymied by unscrupulous scripted instructions. Worst of all, greed for money and lust for power is transforming public schools and public education into political predatory industrial complexes by special interest individuals and groups. Tragically, quality education is not their objective. They are motivated by personal profit from the multi-billion-dollar tax supported, compulsive school attendance educational system. Why teach? You must teach. We are in a raging warfare that we cannot afford to lose. We teachers and parents are fighting for the minds, souls; spirits, bodies, lives and survival values of our children, ourselves, our nation and our world. Quality education rights are more serious than Civil Rights. The right to a quality education is connected with human survival Rights. Teaching in the educational war zone is a duty and a must. We must reclaim, under God, our educational system.

Teach Them Living Skills and Salvation Values

The public schools must major in the teaching of critical specified education, designed for victorious civilized living. The educational curriculum from K-12 must equip each student with optimum skills for making a good life and productive living. In addition to the basics of reading, writing, arithmetic, STEM and STEAM, the students must also be taught biblical literacy, health literacy, socio-economic-political literacy, family values and the skills and competencies to make an honest livelihood in a free society. All children must be taught that they are special because they are made in the image of God. They must be taught the Commandment to love God with all their mind, heart, soul and strength and their neighbor as self. An education for living is a civil and human right of every child. It is criminal negligence and violation of God's Commandments to deprive a child of educational values and the knowledge of God. SOCIETY CAN NO LONGER AFFORD EDUCATIONAL LEADERS WHO FAIL OUR CHILDREN, PUBLIC EDUCATION AND SOCIETY.

The Educational Duty of the Church

Our children are headed back to the public schools to be inundated with STEM education. Science, Technology, Engineering and Math will be the major educational priorities. STEM does not Address the educational values of CARE. The components of C.A.R.E education includes Character, Art, Religious and Ethical education. Many educational districts are depriving children of CARE education. STEM education does not provide for moral guidance and the spiritual virtues of justice, righteousness, love, faith, freedom and hope. The deprivation of CARE education to our children is socially irresponsible, criminally negligent, dis obedient to God and dangerous to civilization. The deprivation of CARE education sets our children up for failure and self-destruction. The Church and Christian believers cannot afford to sit back and be complicit in this colossal crime against our children and humanity. We must use all the resources at our disposal to get CHARACTER, ART, RELIGIOUS, and ETHICAL education in the public schools, beginning with the Atlanta Public Schools of Atlanta, GA.

Back to School with Purpose

We must encourage our children to aim for excellence as they return to school. Our children and ourselves must not allow anything to distract chem from their educational a top priority. Students must not indulge themselves in too much recreation and wasted time. Going to school to learn and achieve academically is serious work. Studying and learning can be satisfying and enjoyable. However, it is not a play thing.

It is serious. Students must realize that God wants them to have knowledge, wisdom and understanding. The Bible teaches us that we, "perish for lack of knowledge." Therefore, we must get as much knowledge as we can in order to live. We must increase our determination to live through knowledge and faith in God. Excellence in education and ethical behavior will help us to be excellent in life for Christ.

Neglected Hearts and social Chaos

The American educational, religious and family institutions are neglecting the nurturing and training of the hearts and spirits of our children. The secular leaders of these institutions prohibit the teaching of character education, ethics, morals, patriotism and the Bible. The secular leaders of these institutions reject spiritual values and the reality of God. These anti-God, anti-Bible and anti-Christ materialistic leaders are cutting off the lifeline of God to the minds, hearts and spirits of our children and others under their influence. They are blocking the door way of God. We must be alarmed and so infuriated that we will take legal action against them to open up the doorway of God for our children. The consequence of this cruel misguided blockage of the doorway to God, is spiritual and moral deprivation that breeds mental illness, spiritual wickedness, crime, and social chaos. Social chaos is increasing because individual internal controls are being diminished by neglected hearts and spirits and the prohibition against God. Civilized societies are based on control from within the individual and not from the outside by police and dictatorial secular authority.

Mind Care Through Love

Let this mind be in you, which was also in Christ Jesus.
(Philippians 2:5)

For who hath known the mind of the Lord, that he may Instruct him? But we have the mind of Christ.
(1Corinthians 2:16)

Jesus said unto him, thou shalt love the Lord thy God With all thy heart, and with all thy soul and with all thy mind.
(Matthew 22:37)

Beloved, let us love one another; for love is of God; And everyone that loveth is born of God, and knoweth God. He that loveth not knoweth not God; for God Is love.
(1John 4:7-8)

Avoid Foolishness and be Wise

The words of Jesus, "Behold, I send you forth as sheep in the midst of wolves: be ye therefore wise as serpents, and harmless as doves." (Matthew 10:1) Jesus admonishes his disciples to be WISE. You must be wise in a world that uses wickedness in high places to do evil. This means that the fight is not just against foolishness, but it is against sophisticated deceptions by persons with advanced education. In order for sheep to survive in the midst of wolves they must be wise. Foolishness is wasteful and destructive. The Bible warns against tools and foolishness with approximately 200 references, mostly in the book of Proverbs. God does not want his children to be foolish. Therefore, God has provided approximately 500 references in the Bible on wisdom and being wise. God's KNOWLEDGE keeps us from perishing. God's WISDOM enables us to discern and choose that which is good, righteous, just and loving. Foolishness is the opposite of wisdom. Foolishness often does great harm. PRAY TO GOD FOR THE GIFT WISDOM.

Your Most Important Priority
Study the Word of God

God has sent a personal message to all the people of the earth. The message is plain. It is in a book known as The Bible. It is written in your language. It is an urgent message. Jeremiah 22: 29, cries out, "O Earth, Earth, Earth, hear the Word of the LORD." Isaiah exclaims, "Hear O Heavens, and give ear, O Earth; for the LORD has spoken." "My Word that goes forth out of my mouth shall not return unto me void (Isaiah 55:11)." Luke 11:28 says, "Blessed are they that hear the Word of God, and keep it." God's Word in the Holy Bible and the Word that "became flesh and dwelt among us," in Jesus Christ is the most important for every living soul. "Thy Word is a lamp unto my feet and a light unto my pathway (Psalm 119:105)." God's Word is" the Way, the Truth and the life." God's Word is light, Knowledge, Wisdom and Understanding God's Word is our lifeline for Salvation. 2 Timothy 2:15, " Study to show thyself approved unto God, a workman that needeth not to be ashamed, rightly dividing the word of truth."

Make Biblical Knowledge A Top Priority

During this season of education and graduations, let us pause to thank God for the HOLY BIBLE that contains the accumulated wisdom of the ages. It is the universal Book that speaks to all humanity, every man, woman and child. It is the Book with messages and GOOD NEWS from God. It is the greatest news that has ever been shared on the planet earth. It is the GOOD NEWS OF GOD AND JESUS CHRIST, HIS SON. The Bible is a book of light and enlightenment and life, itself. The Bible contains the most vital know ledge for every human being. It is food for the body, mind, soul and spirit. The Bible is truth about God and God's WILL for mankind. It gives direction and purpose for every Life. THE WORLD IS PERISHING FOR THE LACK OF BIBLICAL KNOWLEDGE. WE MUST MAKE BIBLE STUDY A TOP PRIORITY. Let us make Bible Study a top priority in the Church, in the homes and everywhere there are people.

Ways to Know the Bible

It is a tragedy to live and die and not know the Word of God in the Bible. There are a number of ways that you can know the Bible. One way is to select a book of the Bible and study it slowly, faithfully and thoroughly. There are sixty-six books in the Old Testament and the New Testament. Another way to know the Bible, is to study about certain characters in the Bible. There are many interesting and fascinating characters in the Bible, beginning with Adam and Eve. There are many others, such as Abraham, Isaac, Jacob, Esau, Joseph, Noah, Moses, King David, Ruth, Samson, Samuel and many others in the Old Testament. The Old Testament is about the history of Israel. Jesus Christ is the central character (the Savior) of the New Testament. There are many other characters in the New testament that are Interesting. Another way of knowing the Bible is to study the Events of the Bible, such as the creation, the flood, tower of Babel and the crossing of the Red Sea, The birth, crucifixion, resurrection and ascension of Jesus. Study the beauty of the Psalms, the wisdom of Proverbs and the suffering of Job. Study the life and teachings of Jesus.

Christian Education for the Public Good

We must encourage the incorporation of Biblical knowledge, character education, civil and ethical learning in our public and private educational systems for the public good. Christian education is that education that undergirds and supports all other legitimate and valid education in the Church and community. We are doing great harm to our children and Nation by not requiring Christian education in our school systems. Christian education provides the proper ethical and moral guidance and equitable regulation of all other values and services in the society. Christianity is the guiding and enlightening force for the safe and constructive use of technology in a civilized and humane society. Christianity is universal and inclusive of all people. Jesus Christ is the only universal Savior of the world. How can anyone justify the deprivation of the Good News of Jesus Christ, who is life, truth and the way?

Character Education Transforms Culture

PARENTS with good character will teach their children the highest and most noble values for success. MEMBERS OF FAMILIES with good character will love, respect and enhance family members for unity. TEACHERS with good character will transmit to their student's true knowledge, humane and survival values. An EDUCATOR with good character, plants truth, knowledge, wisdom and sound doctrines into the learners, institutions, society and culture. The ARTIST with good character will create, express and spread elevated thoughts of beauty and goodness into the minds, hearts and culture of the people of God. The SCIENTIST with good character will invent methods and instruments to help human life and advance civilization. The LAWYER with good character will not compromise truth or justice or go against God's divine laws. The MINISTER with good character will teach, preach, witness, share the good news of God in Christ and be a member of the of the vanguard of truth for the good of civilization. The LEADERS of men and nations must be led by the undeviating will of God found in the Character of Jesus Christ.

Major in Character Education

The American educational system, and especially the public schools, must begin to major in character education to save our youth and the Nation. Character education is the teaching and the transmission of the universal core moral, ethical and spiritual values for the benefit of humanity and for the common good of society. Character education teaches reverence for God, the Creator, and respect for the sacredness and dignity of human Life. The objective of character education is to instill into the human personalities, validated sound core values of justice, righteousness and compassion for human life, civilized society and an enriched culture. There are growing secular influences in America and throughout the world that are discouraging the cultivation of moral, ethical and spiritual values. Sinister efforts are operating to eliminate the Bible, Jesus Christ and God from society. This trend of darkness must be resisted and defeated.

The State of Georgia passed a law (House Bill 605) on April 23, 1999, mandating local boards of education to implement comprehensive Character Education Programs for levels kindergarten through twelve to begin the 2000-2001 school year. The law required the development of the following character traits: courage, patriotism, citizenship, honesty, fairness, respect for others, kindness, cooperation, self-respect, courtesy, compassion, tolerance, diligence, generosity, punctuality, creativity, sportsmanship, loyalty, perseverance, cleanliness, cheerfulness, school pride, respect for environment, respect for Creator, self-control, patience and virtue. (THIS LAW MUST BE ENFORCED!)

Education has A Responsibility to Educate

Due to the vast knowledge meltdown, cultural impoverishment, ethical decline and spiritual wickedness, it is important for educational institutions (including Atlanta Public Schools), to use access TV and other media channels to provide consistent quality educational presentations for the students as well as for the general pub lie. Instead of celebratory and self-promoting TV presentations, TV access channels provide an excellent opportunity to provide a quality of TV education that will benefit students with their academic subjects in science, math, literature and other subjects. Currently, the TV airtime is grossly wasted. Additionally, educational institutions have an opportunity to feature helpful education on the following subjects: (1) U.S. Constitution (2) American Government (3) Cultural Enrichment (4) Professional Ethics (5) Social Justice (6) Sacred, Classical and Negro Spirituals (7) Enhancing Human Life Through Science (8 Ethical Guides for Technology (9) The Rules of Just Laws (10) Respect for Life and God's Creation (11) Human Life and Cultural Diversity (12) Geography, Globalism and Universality. The preceding topics represent a few ideas that could elevate and enhance the benefits of educational TV access.

CORE CURRICULUM FOR EDUCATIONAL SUCCESS
The Institute of Public Theology

I. Education for Justice, Law, Order, Peace, Prosperity

1. Divine Law
2. Natural Law
3. Statutory Law
4. Human and Civil Rights
5. Democratic Government
6. Citizenship Responsibility
7. Patriotic Education
8. United States Constitution
9. American Government
10. Patriotic Values - American Patriotic Values
11. National Security - Survival Values
12. Public Safety and Crime Free Community

II. Education for Civilized Human Behavior

1. Personal Behavioral Accountability
2. Character Education
3. Biblical History and Literature
4. Values Clarification
5. Conflict Resolution
6. Theological Education
7. Christian Education
8. Major World Religions Education
9. Religious Education
10. Ethical, Moral and Spiritual Domains of Learning
11. Cognitive, Affective, Psychomotor Learning Domains

12. Ethical Leadership Foundations

III. Education for Ethical Professionalism

1. The Significance of Professionalism
2. Efficacy of Professional Standards
3. Codes of Morality, Ethics and Humanitarianism
4. Business Ethics, Efficiency, Grievance Procedures
5. Business Education for Common Good
6. Cost Benefit Analysis
7. Ethical Systems of Merit
8. Conflict Resolution for Justice
9. Professional Conduct- "First, Do No Harm"
10. Professional Attire - Dress for Success
11. The Free Enterprise System
12. Business Incorporation as Legal Entity

CORE CURRICULUM FOR EDUCATIONAL SUCCESS
The Institute of Public Theology

IV. Education for Holistic Health

1. Personal Health Education
2. Mental, Physical, Social, Public Health
3. Family Values of Benevolent Caring and Support
4. Remedial Services for Restoration
5. Case Management Services and Community Resources
6. Health Maintenance Services and Community Directories

7. Childcare Protective and Developmental Services
    Family Counseling and Resource Centers
8. Fellowship Support and Growth Groups
9. Substance Abuse Education and Counseling
10. Drug Addiction, Treatment and Prevention
11. Employment Assistance and Training Program

V. STEM EDUCATION
(Science, Technology, Engineering, Math)

VI.   Vocational Educational and Self-Employment
VII. School of Creative Arts Education
VIII. School of Compensatory Education
IX.   Cultural Enrichment Education
X.   Black American Heritage Education and Music
XI.   Journalism and Entertainment Academy
XII. School of Sports and Martial Arts

This Comprehensive Core Curriculum of Education is recommended generally and specifically for the American Public Schools in response to the unprecedented corrosive cultural challenges in America and American Educational Institutions. These unprecedented challenges impact every area of American life. It is urgent and critical that they are met with utmost priority and commitment.

The Institute of Public Theology
P. O. Box 3148
Atlanta, GA 30302

EDUCATION PROHIBITED BY RELIGIOUS DEFINITION
The Bible Defies Constitutional Religion Clause
The Christian Institute of Public Theology

The nebulous definitions, meanings and connotations of religion as used in the First Amendment of the United States Constitution, arbitrarily, mischaracterizes the Bible as a part of the nebulous meaning of religion; and subsequently prohibits the unique, inexhaustible, educational, cultural, historical, social, legal and theological values of the Bible. The Bible is not ordinary, general or nebulous in its description. The Bible is not synonymous with religion as presumed in the First Amendment of the United States Constitution's "religion establishment clause."

The Bible Is a distinct, unique and specific historical, legal, ethical, theological composition of sixty-six specifically named books; combining the Old and New Testament Eras of Jewish History. It covers the whole spectrum of life from Genesis to Revelation in the New Testament. The Old Testament contains 39 books; five books of law; twelve books of history; five books of wisdom and poetry; five books of major prophets; twelve books of minor prophets. The New Testament contains 27 books: four books of Gospels, one book of history, twenty-one letters, and one book of Revelation.

It must be acknowledged that the Bible is not a book of sectarianism, cultism or any ism that is less than monotheism. It is not a book of fiction or mythology or perceptual creations of the imagination. The Bible is a unique historical book that reveals and represents historically, one monotheistic God, one humanity, one Savior. It teaches exclusively of the existence of one omnipotent, omnipresent, omniscient, infinite, immortal and eternal God. The Bible teaches further that the worship of any entity or being less than God is idolatry. There is only one God with the capital G according to the Bible. The polytheistic gods with the small g are idols and are not the monotheistic God of Abraham, Isaac and Jacob. This God resurrected Jesus Christ from the dead. The Bible teaches against religious idolatry. The God of the Bible is the God of love and truth.

DEFINITIONS OF RELIGIONS:

The World Book Dictionary (1998, World Book, Inc) provides four credible definitions of religion as follows: (1) Belief in God or gods. (2) Worship of God or gods. (3) A particular system of religious belief. (4) Anything done or followed with reverence and devotion. These described academic and professional definitions of religion from the World Book Dictionary illustrate the expansive, general and broad definitions of religion. These general and nebulous definitions of religion clearly raise the question as to how can the specificity of the Bible and its criticisms of idolatry and dishonesty be considered as any part of a false and idolatrous religion. The Bible is not synonymous with God. It is not a book to be worshipped. It is not a being that worships. It is not a being that follows. The Bible is not a being that devotes or reveres. The Bible is not a religion. It is a book of history, knowledge, education, truth, God's love, historical acts and instructions for the salvation of mankind.

THE NATURE OF RELIGION MERITS SERIOUS STUDY:

The four definitions of religion by World Book Dictionary are connected and related to personal and individual beliefs, worship, reverence preferences and devotions by individual decisions and choices from a universe of things, objects and beings. The core meaning of religion seems to reside in the personal feelings, belief systems and choices of the respective individuals or groups. Based on the limited information provided, a rational analysis must conclude that the Bible is not a religion. Contrarily, anything can be considered religious. Therefore, the government cannot be isolated from the definition and concept of religion. Based on the nebulous definition of religion, the U.S. Constitution and the American Government, itself, could be considered a religion.

The Bible, itself, proclaims that the worship of anything less than God is idolatry. Human beings adore, reverence and worship a variety of things, objects and beings. Religion appears to originate and reside in the minds, hearts, spirits, souls and the will of individuals and groups as they focus on objects of devotion, reverence and worship. These objects, things or beings are not necessarily specifically limited or defined. The conglomerate complexities of religion and the associated consequences must not be taken lightly. Serious attention is Needed.

REVISITING THE RELIGION ESTABLISHMENT CLAUSE:

The Religion Establishment Clause is based on the First Amendment of the US Constitution. The Religion Establishment Clause is used as the legal basis to prohibit the

Bible from being taught in the government public schools in America. This law is used to justify the prohibition of Bibles and use of Bibles in government agencies and other places of public accommodations; such as hotels and motels. The words, quotations and references to the Bible are often censured, discouraged and disparaged. Some candidates who are being sworn in for American public office refuse to place their hand on the Bible for the administration of the oath of office. The legal restrictions and public prohibitions against the Bible and the use and content of the Bible are being done without sufficient competent legal. investigation and study. Al serious revisit of this "Religion Establishment Clause" is urgently needed. In addition to reviewing the legality of the "Religion Establishment Clause," competent social, national, political, economic, cultural, health, educational and theological impact study would be of great service to America and the world. The heterogeneous and technological complexities of the world have critically, narrowed the margins of error. This error is unaffordable.

THE READING AND LANGUAGE OF THE FIRST AMENDMENT OF THE U.S. CONSTITUTION:

"Congress shall make no law respecting an establishment of religion, or prohibiting the free exercise thereof; or abridging the freedom of speech, or of the press; of the right of the people peaceably to assemble, and to petition the government for a redress of grievances."

THE CONSTITUTION OF THE UNITED STATES OF AMERICA

RELATIONSHIP OF THE BIBLE TO AMERICAN LAW:

The influence of the Bible predates the 13 American Colonies that began about 1607 AD. Christian ministers and other Christians spread the teaching of the Bible throughout the Thirteen Colonies in America. The spread of the teachings of the Bible and the salvation news of Jesus Christ brought about eventually, what is called the "Great Awakening" in the American Colonies. The great spiritual awakening resulted from a massive Christian led movement of evangelistic teachings, revivals, conversions and dedication to freedom to live, work and worship without government restrictions and hindrance. It must be noted that Black Africans (Negro slaves) were first brought to the Colony at Jamestown, Virginia in 1619 and they were not considered as fully equal or equally human as their White counterparts. However, they became a part of this vibrant social and political movement in the new colonial world.

The culture of the Colonies became saturated with the ethical teachings, enlightening know ledge and liberating spirit of the biblical knowledge of the Bible and the soul salvation know ledge of Jesus Christ. The Colonists were inspired and motivated to build communities, churches and schools and to engage in free enterprise endeavors. This new beginning was inspired and sustained by the Christians and Bible believers. The Bible was their primary reading and teaching book. Many could not read or write, but they learned through the oral quotations of Scripture of the Bible. The Bible became a motivator to learn to read, write and get an education. Many schools were established during this colonial period. Many African American slaves were motivated to read and get an education so that they could read the Bible. The American Negro slaves never considered the Bible a "White man's religion."

It was the influence of the Bible that initiated the Declaration of Independence in 1776; the Constitution of the United States in 1787. The Bible influenced the ratification of the Bill of Rights in 1791and the recognition of a democratic form of government described by President Abraham Lincoln in 1863 as, "a government of the people, by the people, and for the people," and the issuance of the Emancipation Proclamation in 1863 that freed the Negro American slaves in 1863. In subsequent years the Bible influenced the Pledge of Allegiance to the U.S. Flag as "One Nation under God." and the American Motto on American currency, "In God We Trust." The influence of the Bible is imbedded deeply in the American culture, education, social, economic and political institutions. The single most document that has made the greatest difference for good in America and the world, has been and is the Holy Bible. This magnificent, unfathomable and extraordinary gift to humanity must be respected, re-examined, revisited, reconsidered, reunited, reclaimed, replenished, renewed and revitalized. Generations, civilizations and nations have been enlightened, guided, nurtured and strengthened by the knowledge, understanding, wisdom, spiritual concern and love contained in and radiates from the Bible.

EXPLORING THE BIBLICAL AND LEGAL PARADOX:

Considering the massive enlightening and constructive influence of the Bible on the American culture and founding documents and Western Civilization as well; this paradoxical irony must be emphatically noted and explored. It is an egregious ironical paradox that the Religion Establishment Clause of the Fourteenth Amendment of the U.S. Constitution is used (paradoxically) to prohibit the Bible from being taught in the public government schools, along with disparaging attempts to build a wall of separation between the Bible and the government; cloaked as "separation of government and religion," and " separation of "Church and State," How is this rational, legitimate and reconcilable when the unique Bible has been influencing cultures, civilization and nations for civility and good for over five thousand years? Biblical knowledge and the foundation and guidance for the governing documents, the Constitution and the democracy of America are based on biblical influence. The Bible is the foundation for America's Constitution, Democracy and civilization's humanizing influence.

The disparagement, marginalization and misrepresentation of the Bible, in reference to the "Religion Establishment Clause" is based on dogmatic ignorance of the Bible's manifested significant truths and prolife human values for over five thousand years of world history. The expansive disparagement and prohibitions against the Bible is also based on the false premises and presumptions that the Bible is a religion (undefined). The disparagement and subservient relegated status of the Bible in the American Government and general society, has and continues to cause tragic human deprivations, cultural damages, political corruption and national calamities beyond description and calculations.

APPEAL, REQUEST AND RECOMMENDATION:

IT IS HEREBY APPEALED, REQUESTED AND HEREBY RECOMMENDED BY THE DULY INCORPO RATED CHRISTIAN INSTITUE OF PUBLIC THEOLOGY OF THE STATE OF GEORGIA, USA

TO: THE PRESIDENT OF THE UNITED STATES; UNITED STATES CONGRESS: THE UNITED STATES SUPREME COURT

IT IS RESPECTFULLY REQUESTED THAT THE APPROPRIATE AGENCIES OF THE AMERICAN GOVERNMENT:

DEFINE THE MEANING AND ROLE OF RELIGION IN THE FIRST AMENDMENT OF THE CONSTITUTION OF THE UNITED STATES.

CLARIFY THE LEGAL PLACE, PUBLIC ROLE, EDUCATIONAL CLASSIFICATION, THE RELATIONSHIP OF THE GOVERNMENT TO THE BIBLE AS RELATED TO THE FIRST AMENDMENT TO THE CONSTITUTION OF THE UNITED STATES OF AMERICA.

The Christian Institute of Public Theology, Inc

EDUCATIONAL RESOURCES FOR THE ABUNDANT LIFE
Names for Educational Institutions and Courses of Study

Recommended Names for Theological Educational Institution:

1. LIFE VALUES INSTITUTE
2. LIFE EDUCATIONAL VALUES INSTITUTE
3. LEADERSHIP FOR LIFE INSTITUTE
4. EDUCATIONAL VALUES FOR LIVING ACADEMY
5. VALUES FOR LIVING INSTITUTE
6. HUMAN LIFE EDUCATIONAL VALUES ACADEMY
7. RESOURCES FOR LIVING INSTITUTE
8. THE INSTITUTE OF HUMAN VALUES
9. THE INSTITUTE FOR HUMAN VALUES
10. THE INSTITUTE OF VALUES FO LIVING
11. HUMAN LIFE VALUES INSTITUTE
12. ABUNDANT LIFE EDUCATIONAL INSTITUTION
13. EDUCATIONAL INSTITUTION FOR LIVING
14. HUMAN REFINEMENT SANCTUARY
15. HUMAN REFINEMENT ACADEMY
16. THE CULTURAL ENRICHMENT CENTER
17. CULTIVATING SENTIMENTS FOR LIVING ACADEMY
18. CULTIVATING NURTUING SENTIMENTS CENTER
19. THEOLOGY FOR CIVILIZATION INSTITUTE
20. THE CHARACTER EDUCATION INSTITUTE
21. THE SPIRITUAL DOMAIN INSTITUTE
22. SPIRITUAL EDUCATION ACADEMY
23. BIBLICAL KNOWLEDGE INSTITUTE
24. UNIVERSAL SALVATION KNOWLEDGE CENTER
25. THE HUMAN REDEMPTION CENTER
26. THE HUMANIZING VALUES SCHOOL
27. TRANSFORMING KNOWLEDGE & SPIRIT CENTER
28. SALVATION VALUES FOR LIFE ACADEMY

29. THE CIVILIZING AND HUMANIZING INSTITUTE
30. THE LIFE HUMANIZING VALUES INSTITUTION
31. THE NEW BIRTH EDUCATIONAL CENTER
32. THE GRATITUDE CENTER FOR GOD'S GIFTS
33. FOR GOD SO LOVED THE WORLD SANCTUARY

CHAPTER 9
SALVATION IN JESUS CHRIST

GOD'S GREATEST REVELATION OF LOVE

God sent his Son into the world to save you and me. He can come no closer to us than he has already come. He was made flesh. He was born of a woman. He dwelt among us for thirty-three years. He paid the ultimate sacrificial price for our sins on Calvary's Cross. He was subjected to the cruel crucifixion on a cross by the dark ignorance and wickedness of this world. This crime was not done in secret. It was public historic spectacle in- broad day light. However, it turned dark at high noon. It is recorded in history. However, on the third day, He was resurrected from the dead to live forever more. The resurrection was not a secret. It happened. It is historical. The record is clear and replete. In addition to the Gospels, Matthew, Mark, Luke and John; there is a list of a, "Cloud of Witnesses," proclaiming that JESUS LIVES as a RISEN SAVIOR. It is utmost tragic to disavow and ignore the coming of our LORD and SAVIOR.

The Reconciling Spirit

The Spirit of Christ reconciles differences, diversity and divisions. Humanity is torn asunder with alienating divisions. Humanity is fragmented and weakened by these divisions. These divisions create conflict, confusion, hostilities and warfare. Brothers and sisters, men and women, races and nations become enemies to each other. Humanity, itself, forfeits the great joys and blessings of God with the preoccupation of hatred and division. There is hope! The Spirit of Christ has the power to reconcile diverse and hostile spirits. It is the will of God that men, women, boys and girls live in peace all over the world. Alienating spirits do not want peace. The ungodly spirits are disobedient and in rebellion against God. They have an unhealthy, blind and sick need for division, hatred and evil. Their influence and leader ship can lead to violence, destruction and death. God's plea to all mankind is: "Peace," "Love," "Joy," "Goodwill," in your hearts, minds, spirits, souls and world. Let there be peace within and peace outside.

Jesus Christ Is Real in History

There is more evidence and proof of the reality of Jesus Christ in world history than any other individual who has ever lived. The historical record is clear, that Jesus was born to Mary and Joseph in Bethlehem in the year 1 A.D. He lived an active, eventful, miraculous life for 33 years in history. He was crucified in history at Calvary. He was resurrected from the dead on the 3rd day, which was on Sunday, the 1st day of the week. Jesus showed himself alive for forty days by many infallible proofs before he was taken up in a cloud as his disciples watched him disappear from their sight (Acts 1:9-12). Jesus is the child that was born and the Son that was given (Isaiah 9:6). Jesus was the Word that was made flesh and dwelt among us (John 1:14). His name is above every name, whether they be presidents, kings, judges, popes, priests or prophets. The Bible says, "Wherefore God also has highly exalted him, and given him a name which is above every name (Philippians 2:9). Jesus not only lived in history, but he is also the single Individual who is at the center of history, BC and AD. He was Born in history, lived in history, crucified in history, resurrected in History and ascended in history. HE LIVES!

Jesus Is Knowable and Available

Jesus Christ is knowable and available. There is a long list of witnesses in every generation for two thousand years who profess to know Jesus. Jesus is knowable and available for each individual in every generation for two thousand years and at this present time. Jesus is knowable. Each person who seeks, asks and knocks at the door, will find, receive and enter in the Spiritual Domain of Jesus Christ. Jesus is knowable. Are you seeking to know Jesus, who he is? Millions have sought and found him. Millions of diverse, blind, deaf, lame, hungry, lost, heartbroken, demonic, diseased, rejected, lonely people have gotten to know Jesus. Jesus is knowable and accessible. It is good to know Jesus through others. However, It is vital to know Jesus for yourself. Seek ye the Lord while he may be found and worship him while he is near. There is none other name under heaven given among men whereby we must be saved. JESUS IS KNOWABLE AND APPROACHABLE!

The Body of Jesus Christ

The Church represents the Body of Jesus Christ. The Body of Jesus Christ is a Body of Love. This Body of Love is a fellowship of Believers who accommodate whosoever will, let him or her come. In this Body of Love, there is room for repentance and forgiveness. There is room for goodness and mercy. There is room for justice and righteousness. There is room for joy and beauty. There is room for peace and goodwill. There is room for brotherhood and sisterhood. There is room for truth, knowledge, wisdom and understanding. There is room for meditation, prayer and worship. There is room for preaching and teaching the Gospel. There is room for serving our sisters and brothers to the glory of God. However, there is no room for hatred and wickedness in the Body of Christ and in the hearts and lives of God's people.

God's Spiritual Connection with Man

Spirituality is the moral, intellectual, emotional and autonomous capacity of the human being to relate to the spiritual attributes of God. The spiritual attributes of God include love, truth, goodness, faith, hope, compassion and beauty. Spirituality is the essence of the image, likeness and nature of God. "They that worship God, must worship him in spirit and in truth." Spirituality is the relating connection between God and man. When the spiritual capacity of man is empty, disconnected or dormant, life loses its significance and purpose. This disconnection from God allows alien and evil spirits to dwell in the capacity meant for God's spirit to dwell. Hearts harboring evil spirits begin to rebel, destroy and self-destruct. ANY PERSON, SYSTEM OR PHILOSOPHY THAI HINDERS ANY PERSON, AND ESPECIALLY CHILDREN, FROM THE CAPACITY TO CONNECT WITH GOD, IS EVIL AND ANTI-CHRIST. We must seriously evaluate laws, persons and institutions that hinders the human connection with God.

JESUS CHRIST IS THE RISEN SAVIOR

JESUS CHRIST, the SAVIOR of the world, is the greatest news to ever come to the planet earth. Jesus comes with truth, eternal life, the way to God, spiritual light, light of the world, love, wisdom, knowledge, authority, healing, mercy and forgiveness. He came in the flesh as Mary's Baby. He was and is the Word that was made flesh (and dwelt among us), lived, grew, crucified on a cross, buried, resurrected, commissioned his disciples and ascended to live forevermore. The additional good news is, that this truth is recorded in human history with invincible evidence and infallible proofs. It was the single event that split the history of the world into BC (Before Christ) and AD (In the year of our Lord). That is how and why we arrive at today's date. If you have heard and received this GOOD NEWS, you are required to go and share it with others. Go Tell It on The Mountain. Tell it in the valleys. Tell the GOOD NEWS to family, colleagues, neighbors, friends and foes. Tell it to the churches, schools and every segment of the community. Tell it with your voice, pen and paper, by mail and email, the telephones, smart phones, the internet and social media, that JESUS CHRIST is come!

The Value of Freedom

Thousands upon thousands of people have sacrificed and died to pass on a legacy of freedom. And yet, so many are still not free. Many have not kept Freedom alive. Many have enslaved themselves by choosing to be ignorant. They enslave themselves to drugs, crime, jealousy, arrogance, greed, foolish ness and stupidity. Some have enslaved themselves through slothfulness, indifference and passivity.

Some have allowed others to enslave them because they rejected knowledge, enlightenment and God. Hosea says, "My people are destroyed for lack of knowledge." Isaiah says, "My people are gone into captivity because they have no knowledge."(Isaiah 5:13) Knowledge is knowing the truth. More specifically, it is knowing the truth of God. Jesus declares that he is the way, the truth and the life. Allow God to make you his captive, and you will be free. Let us not take freedom for granted. We must hold on to freedom through knowledge and struggle and pass the legacy of freedom to our children and the oncoming generations.

Have You Accepted Your Identity in Jesus Christ?

God has given you an identity in the household of faith. Have you accepted and adopted your spiritual identity in Jesus Christ? In the book of Genesis God shows human favor by creating the man and the woman in his image. That is good news for man. Receive that good news. YOU ARE CREATED IN THE IMAGE OF GOD.I God also gave man dominion over every other creature of the earth. The Psalmist teaches that God is mindful of man and has crowned him with glory and honor and has put all things under his feet. The First Book of Peter identifies the believers as a "chosen generation," a holy nation," a "royal priesthood," "peculiar people," called out of darkness into God's marvelous light as a people of God who have obtained mercy. God so loved man (the world) that he gave his Only Begotten Son and makes it possible for man to become a "new creature in Christ and the inheritor of eternal life. What is your identity without Christ? What is your future without Christ? can you afford to be without Christ? What a gift; what an honor; what a privilege and a blessing to have the spiritual identity of Jesus Christ!

The God Ordained Leader

God does not want his people to be lost in darkness, con fusion, ignorance and death. God provides true enlightened leadership for all humanity that leads ultimately to the abundant and eternal life in Jesus Christ. This invitation to follow Jesus is extended to all people. Jesus declares, "I am 'the way, the truth and the life (John 14:6)." "Come unto me all we that labor and are heavy laden, and I will give you rest. (Matthew 11:28)." Who are you following? Who are your leaders following? It is unwise, dangerous and destructive to follow a leadership that does not follow Jesus Christ. It is your duty to find out who you are following. You may be headed in the wrong direct ion. Proverbs 16:25 says that here is a way that seems right unto a man but the end thereof are the ways of death. God has given mankind a righteous leader of life who is Jing of kings, Lord of lords, Prince of peace, the Mighty God and the resurrected Savior. Jesus Christ is God's ordained leader for Humanity acts 4:12 says, "for there is none other name under heaven given among men whereby we must be saved."

Believe on Jesus Today

Every person needs the Savior. Many people search for salvation through religion, church, government, various shrines, ideologies, philosophies and doctrines. Some religions and ideologies have positive benefits and helpful services for human life and society. However, the research shows clearly that there is no salvation in any religion or other manmade institution. Salvation is found only in God through Jesus Christ. History has not revealed another resurrected savior other than Jesus Christ. Jesus is well documented in history and the Scripture as being the Savior of the world (John 3:16). It is explicitly stated in Acts: "NEITHER ISTHERE SALVATION IN ANY OTHER: FOR THERE IS NONE OTHER NAME UNDER HEAVEN GIVEN AMONG MEN, WHERE BY WE MUST BE SAVED."

(Acts 4:12)

Whoever you are, believe on the Lord Jesus Christ today. Tomorrow may be too late. "How shall we escape, if we neglect so great salvation."

(Hebrews 2:3)

Accept God's Plan for Your Life

Be fruitful, positive, multiply, replenish the earth; subdue it and have dominion over all creatures. Love God and your neighbor as yourself. Do good, walk humbly, be merciful and forgiving. Render to all their dues; respect, tribute, custom and honor. Owe no one anything and love one another. Study to show yourself approved unto God, rightly dividing the Word of truth. Be not conformed to this world, but be you transformed by the renewing of your mind. Let not your heart be troubled, believe in God and his Only Begot ten Son, Jesus Christ. Let your light shine before men that they may see your good works and glorify God in heaven. Pray without ceasing. Endure hardship as a good soldier of Jesus Christ.
Fight the good fight, finish your course and keep the faith. Be strong in the Lord and the power of his might. Put on the whole armor of God. Fret not yourself because of evil doers.

Accept God's plan for your life and claim victory in Jesus Christ.

How to be Saved

According to the Scripture: "That if thou shall confess with thy Mouth the Lord Jesus, and shall believe in thy heart that God Has raised him from the dead, thou shall be saved."

(Romans 10:9)

The Scriptures make very clear that we are saved by faith in Jesus Christ through the grace of the loving God.

(John 3:16)

The Scriptures also make clear that there is salvation in no Other except Jesus Christ:

"Neither is their salvation in any other: For there is none other Name under heaven given among men, whereby we must be Saved."

(Acts 4:12)

HOW SHALL WE ESCAPE IF WE NEGLECT SO GREAT SALVATION:
(Foundation: Educating the people of God)

Finally, my brethren, be strong in the Lord, and in the power of his might. Put on the whole armour of God, that you may be able to stand against the wiles of the devil.

For we wrestle not against flesh and blood, but against principalities, against powers, against the rulers of the darkness of this world, against spiritual wickedness in high places.

Wherefore take unto you the whole armour of God, that you may be able to withstand in the evil day, and having done all, to stand.

Ephesians 6:10-13

CHAPTER 10
THEOLOGICAL ETHICS
Greatest Book and Supreme Law

The Word of God in the Bible supersedes the US Constitution and all other manmade laws. The Bible is the Book from God to mankind that has authority and jurisdiction over all mankind in all places and to all generations in heaven and in earth. The hierarchy of Biblical administration is through Jesus Christ, the Holy Spirit and the Church of Christ. The Church receives its orders from God, the Father, Son and Holy Ghost. Every soul is subject unto God God's message Is for every person and every nation. The people of God and che Church bow only unto God. God requires all persons and all nations to bow to God. This includes all kings, emperors, queens, presidents, supreme courts, leaders, constitutions and manmade laws. The Bible is superior to the U.S. Constitution and all other manmade laws. All human beings, men and women are first and foremost creatures of God, not of the state, the nation, secular society or any other creature. God is the sole owner of human beings. Therefore, all men and all nations are accountable to God and subject to the Supreme Laws of God, And the consequences for violations.

What Is a True Religion?

A true religion is based on sound and true doctrines and practices that points to, and connects with, the will and reality of God. In true religion, God Is recognized as being omnipotent, omniscient, • omnipresent, infinite, eternal, immortal and Creator. The doctrines, principles and practice of true religion must be congruent and in harmony with the following universal values: LIFE, TRUTH, JUSTICE, GOODNESS, RIGHTEOUSNESS, LOVE, LIGHT, BEAUTY, FAITH AND HOPE. True religion is universally inclusive of all human beings as brothers and sisters under the Fatherhood of God. In true religion God is worshipped in truth and in spirit. True religion allows tor the autonomy of the individuals tree will as opposed to coercive intimidations of the mind and the involuntary servitude of the body. True religion contains redemptive revelations from God that are specifically manifested in a historical context of Invincible evidence and Infallible proof. Remember that religions, prophets, doctrines and principles can be false. Therefore, it is vitally important for everyone to seek, ask, pray and study until you have found TRUE RELIGION THAT OFFERS SALVATION IN JESUS CHRIST.

The Righteousness of God is the Standard

God has already set the standards for his righteousness for all mankind. t is perilous and dangerous to substitute the righteousness of man for the righteousness of God. Therefore, it is a primary responsibility for every person to learn the righteousness of God standards as set by God. This is vitally important because Proverbs 14:12 says, "There is a way which seemeth right unto a man, but the end thereof are the ways of death." Romans 10:2-3 confirms what Proverbs says in the following words, "For I bear them record that they have a zeal of God, but not according to knowledge. For they being ignorant of God's righteousness, and going about to establish their own righteousness, have not submitted themselves unto the righteous ness of God." Religious and political zeal without the righteousness of God and without the knowledge of God's Word, is perilous, deceptive and destructive. When people deviate from the ways of God, like sheep without a shepherd, they go astray. Judges 21:25 gives insight into self-righteousness in the following verse, "In those days there was no king in Israel: every man did that which was right in his own eyes." Thanks be to God for giving humanity a righteous king in Jesus Christ. Follow King Jesus, the Christ.

Judgement Without Truth is Dangerous

If you are not a prophet authorized by God, your pre-judgements without evidence .and factual proof, is not valid, and can be tragic. Matthew 7:1 says, "Judge not, that you be not judged." The premature judgement of others, brings about judgement upon the person who judged others falsely. Gossip and prejudicial judgements are rampant in our society. Irresponsible gossip and hateful judgements not only create unhealthy and dangerous social environments; but they also defame characters, ruin reputations and sometimes cause death. We must use our minds, guard our tongues and let our minds and hearts be led by the Spirit of Christ. We must not be any part of the mob that goes around maliciously, dehumanizing, demonizing, victimizing and killing innocent people. The Black Americans of all others, must not be a part of shutting down free speech in America (as is being done to Donald Trump). We must remember that it was the irrational, prejudicial mob behavior that allowed the known Criminal, Barabbas, to go free, and they shouted out that Jesus, an Innocent man and Savior, be crucified. It is not Trump that they are Attempting to shut down. It is the freedom that Dr. King died for, and THE TRUTH THAT JESUS IS.

Spiritual Discernment is Critical

How do you keep yourself from being deceived by harmful and Ungodly people? How can you safeguard yourself from false information and unsound doctrines? How can you keep yourself from being misled by misleading ideologies? How can you avoid the pitfalls and temptations of seducing spirits? How can you know the right way when there are multiple ways? How can you know the truth when there are so many different opinions and versions? How can you have the assurance that you are being led by truth and the righteousness of God? In answer to these questions, consider the admonition of (1st John 4:1-3):

Beloved, believe not every spirit, but try the spirits whether they are of God: because many false prophets are gone out into the world. Hereby, know ye the Spirit of God: Every spirit that confesses that Jesus Christ is come in the flesh is of God. And every spirit that confesses not that Jesus Christ is come in the flesh is not of God: and this is that spirit of antichrist.

God's Will Is Made Known to Mankind

The Bible contains the Word of God and the Will of God. God's Will is revealed in God's Word. Why do so few people know the Will of God when it is not a secret? God has made his Will known to humanity. God's Will is further revealed in his creation of light, life, truth, justice, goodness, righteousness, love, peace, beauty, mercy, knowledge, wisdom and understanding. God loves humanity so much that he made known his Will, ways, truth, wisdom and understanding to those who seek, ask and knock. God personalizes his Will in Jesus Christ. Jesus Christ is not a secret. His name is exalted above every name. "For God so loved the world, that he gave his Only Begotten Son, that whosoever believeth in should not perish, but have everlasting life (John 3:16)." Jesus Christ is the undeviating Will of God to reach mankind. Jesus is the way, the truth and the life (John 146). It is the duty, honor, privilege and blessing for every person to find out the Will of God for the world and for one's own Life. The revelation of God's Will in Jesus Christ is the best Good News for mankind. How shall we escape if we neglect so great salvation?

(Hebrews2:3)

Believe the Christ Spirit

Beloved, believe not every spirit, but try the spirits whether They are of God: because many false prophets are gone out into the world. Hereby know ye the spirit of God: Every spirit. that confesseth that Jesus Christ is come in the flesh is of God. And every spirit that confesseth not that Jesus Christ is come in the flesh is not of God. And this is that spirit of antichrist, whereof ye have heard that it should come; and even now is it in the world. (1st John 4:1-3)

The Christ Spirit is the most powerful spirit in the world. Because it is the Spirit of God. The Christ Spirit is the Spirit of God. The Christ Spirit is the Christmas Spirit. The Christ Spirit is the Holy Spirit. It is the Spirit of Love. God IS LOVE. The Christ Spirit is the Spirit of Truth, Righteousness, Good ness, Justice and mercy. As the antichrist spirits rise up, and they are; let us be able to recognize them. Antichrist spirits are deceitful, arrogant, negative, weak and evil. Antichrist spirits are antigod and antilife. Do not allow the antichrist spirits to bully you. "Standup, Standup for Jesus, you soldiers of the Cross."

Peace with God

There can be no outside peace without peace within. There can be no peace within without peace with God. The expressions of human conflicts, hatred, injustice, evil, bitterness, wars and destruction are outward manifestations of the rebellious and wicked hearts within. Evil minds and iniquitous hearts sow seeds of evil, confusion and destruction. You cannot have true peace in your life, your home, your school, your church, your business, your society and nation until you have peace within from God. Faith in God through Jesus Christ is the top priority for peace and salvation for every human being. The Bible has 421 references to peace. "Therefore, being justified by faith, we have peace with God through our Lord Jesus Christ." (Romans 5:1) Let there be peace! Let it begin with me and you today!

What Is Your Spiritual (Identification)?

God has given spiritual identification to those who accept him in the beginning, God gives man (includes woman) a positive and Significant identification by creating them in God's image (Gen 1:27). Accepting Jesus Christ as your Lord and Savior, provides you with the spiritual identification of God. Your spiritual identification with God is your most significant identification (1 John 4:1-3). When you accept Jesus Christ as Lord and Savior, you become born Again

(John 3:7) and a new creature (2Cor. 5: 17) in Christ. Your spiritual identification in Christ makes you a part of a chosen generation, a royal priesthood, a holy nation and a peculiar people (1 Peter 2:9-10) called out of darkness into his marvelous light as people of God. Our spiritual identification in Christ brings us near by the blood of Christ (Ephesians 2:13). Therefore, Paul says that we are no longer aliens; we are no more strangers and foreigners, but fellow citizens with the saints, and the household of God (Ephesians 2:19). We are the children of the light and the day (Thessalonians 5:5) not of the night or the darkness. Our spiritual Identification is based on our confession that Jesus is the Son of God and God dwells in him (1 John 4:15) and that God is love and he that dwell in God dwells in love (1 John 4:16).

How to Know God's Will

God's Will is knowable. God has revealed his Will. God has Revealed God's Will in the natural ordered creation. God has revealed God's Will in Biblical Divine Revelations, God has revealed God's Will in Jesus Christ, in studying the handiwork of God's creation you can learn something about the Will of God. In studying God's Word in the Old Testament and in the New Testament God reveals God's Will. In accepting Jesus Christ as your Lord and Savior you can know the Will of God. Jesus Christ is the undeviating Will of God to reach mankind. It is critically important to know God's Will because your life is somewhere in the Will of God. When you learn about God's Will, you are in a better position to know God's Will for your life. It is tragic for the blindness of your will to be contrary to the Will of God. When David learned he was outside the Will of God, he asked God to, "Create in me a clean heart, O God; and renew a right spirit within me." Psalms 51:10. The Bible makes over 870 references to the heart. When God cleans your heart, you will know God's Will.

Focusing on Majors and Priorities

When your leadership is in crisis and your society is in confusion, it is a time to major in top priorities. Challenges for the people of God have never been more serious than they are presently, in this 21st Century. Lostness, darkness and ignorance are rampant in our society. However, there is good news in the Word of God to help us to get back on course of righteousness. There is good news in the Word of God to help us focus on what is important and what our majors and priorities should be. Joshua 24:15 says, "Choose you this day whom you will serve." Jesus says in Matthew 6:33, "But seek you first the kingdom of God, and his righteousness, and all these things shall be added unto you." Seeking the Kingdom first will cause other priorities to find their rightful place. Let us set our focus on double and triple majors and let us teach our children to do the same. Let us major in the following priorities: Knowledge, Wisdom, Understanding, Love, Justice, Peace, Righteousness, Goodness, joy and beauty.

Ways to Know the Bible

It is a tragedy to live and die and not know the Word of God in the Bible. There are a number of ways that you can know the Bible. One way is to select a book of the Bible and study it slowly, faithfully and thoroughly. There are sixty-six books in the Old Testament and the New Testament. Another way to know the Bible, is to study about certain characters in the Bible. There are many interesting and fascinating characters in the Bible, beginning with Adam and Eve. There are many others, such as Abraham, Isaac, Jacob, Esau, Joseph, Noah, Moses, King David, Ruth, Samson, Samuel and many others in the Old Testament. The Old Testament is about the history of Israel. Jesus Christ is the central character (the Savior) of the New Testament. There are many other characters in the New Testament that are Interesting. Another way of knowing the Bible is to study the Events of the Bible, such as the creation, the flood, tower of Babel and the crossing of the Red Sea, The birth, crucifixion, resurrection and ascension of Jesus. Study the beauty of the Psalms, the wisdom of Proverbs and the suffering of Job. Study the life and teachings of Jesus.

The Way from Cultism

The cult mind set and groups are enslaving, divisive and destructive. Cults use non biblical sources of authority and perpetuate false teachings. The sectarian groups refuse to see the whole truth. They see what they want to see to confirm what they want to believe. Cults and sectarian groups teach false doctrines and they are intolerant of the truth. They seek to control others through false beliefs. Their doctrines about life, God, Christ and the Bible are distorted and confused. Cultism and sectarianism perpetuate confusion, conflict and violence. Jesus Christ is the way out of cultism and sectarianism. Jesus is the way, truth and the life. You cannot have a healthy mind by being antichrist. Jesus is the light of the world and he is the Great Physician.

The Fatherhood of God

Jesus Christ personalizes God and connects God to humanity by addressing God as, "Our Father," "The Father" and "Father." Jesus, through love and grace connects God to and with the universal human family as the FATHER of all. God, in Jesus Christ, becomes the loving producer, provider, protector and Savior of mankind. Jesus is good news because he is God News -The ultimate news about God. Jesus is good news to the world through the Father hood of God. Jesus demonstrates through the good news of the. Gospel that God is involved in the agonizing human struggle. The Heavenly Father sends his Only Begotten Son to partner with us in the building of his Kingdom on the earth and to bring salvation to all those who will believe and receive. It is the solemn duty of the earthly fathers and all men to take the leadership in majoring in the serious business of fatherhood and the responsible and Godly rearing of children. It is the solemn duty of every person to support and esteem manhood and fatherhood. The significant roles that men and fathers must carry out have been given and ordained of God. Let us teach all our children at an early age to say, "Our Father, which art in heaven, hallowed be thy name, thy kingdom come ..."

PSYCHOTRAUMA: THE HUMAN

INJUSTICE CRISIS

There is a need to express forcefully, that human injustice is a painful, destructive and lethal social disease. Psychotrauma: The Human Injustice Crisis, is an effort to document the destructive influence of human injustice. There is a direct link between injustice and stress, injustice and violence, injustice and depression. There is a direct link between injustice and homicide, injustice and suicide. The destructive influence of injustice grossly impairs the normal functioning of human individuals. Most significantly, it has been known to transform persons of good moral character into dangerous killers. It is a contagious venomous poison.

Economic deprivation is at the core of the human injustice crisis. Human rights violations involving economic security is the basis of widespread Psychotrauma. Injustice aimed at undermining a person's economic security seems to have the greatest effects in triggering Psychotrauma. Human rights violations involving job rights and property rights are most common precipitators of Psychotrauma. Job rights and property rights appear to be more essential to the individual psychological well-being than what has been previously acknowledged. To deprive a person of his means of livelihood, unjustly, can mean, to deprive a person of his life.

After a thorough examination of the literature, it is concluded that this work is the most complete and comprehensive account of the destructive process of psychotrauma. It reveals the innermost workings of the brain and the mind under extreme psychological pressure. It describes an overload and breakdown of the mind. It illustrates and demonstrates the meaning of the breaking point. For the first time, human injustice is linked to this destructive process. The relationship between injustice and violence is illustrated and dramatized. Injustice is not a passive, covert, benign act. Injustice is an act of violence with legal and criminal implications.

BIBLICAL KNOWLEDGE IS NOT A RELIGION
The Christian Institute of Public Theology

It is tragic that the uninformed notion and misconception that the Bible or Biblical knowledge is a religion and is being erroneously perpetuated and categorized as such. The canonized sixty-six books of the Bible are not a religion. The Bible is a special revelatory history of Israel, and the life, teachings, crucifixion, resurrection and ascension of Jesus Christ in history, along with writings of his followers. The Bible incorporates about four thousand years of Israel's history.

The Bible consists of the world's greatest classical literature. The Old Testament has 5 books of Law, 12 Books of History, 5 Books of Poetry, 5 Books of Minor Prophets and 12 Books of Minor Prophets. The New Testament has 4 Books of the Gospel of Jesus Christ, one Book of Church History, 14 Books of Letters and one Book of Prophecy. These Sixty-Six Canonized Books of the Bible contain the most unique and significant knowledge of history. Their impact and relevance are enduring. The Bible contains the most universal, validated truth, ethical, moral and civilized human survival values known to mankind. These values are not restricted to any religion, ideology, race, nationality, language or culture. The indispensable universal human survival values of the Bible are for all human beings, peoples and nations of the earth.

It must be emphasized that God and religion are not synonymous. Jesus Christ and Christianity are not synonymous. There are many religions (organized, ceremonial, ritualistic worshippers and orders) that incorporate moral, ethical ideologies and philosophies that are positive and helpful for humanity. However, it must be made plain, that salvation does not exist in any religion, Church or organization, however noble they may be. The validated authoritative Bible teaches that there is no salvation in religion, race or nation. None of these things can de liver man from the prison-house of his finiteness, mortality and limited time.

The Book of Acts 4:12, makes it clear in these words, "Neither is their salvation in any other: for there is none other name under heaven given among men whereby we must be saved." The Book of John 3:16, makes the source of salvation explicit in the following words, "For God so loved the world that he gave his Only Begotten Son, that whosoever believeth in him should not perish, but have everlasting life.

CHAPTER 11
GOALS AND THEMES OF
PUBLIC THEOLOGY

Theological Approaches for Cultural Transformation
Foundations for Biblical Exposition
(Christian Institute of Public Theology)

1. Biblical Truth Dissemination
2. Artistic Creations
3. Exemplification of Love
4. Earth Replenishment
5. Ethical Actions
6. Environmental Protection
7. Environmental Safety
8. Ethical Actions
9. Ethical Reformation
10. Esthetics Beauty
11. Equity of Justice
12. Cultured Sociality
13. Civilized Expression
14. Characterization of Goodness
15. Health and Wholeness
16. Humanitarian Innovations
17. Cultural Refinement
18. Decency and Order
19. Revelations of Excellence
20. Reality of Truth
21. Spiritual Discernment
22. Redemptive Human Services
23. Humanization of Technology
24. God's Ethical Standards for Humanity
25. The Universality of Justice
26. Righteousness of God
27. Refinement of Humanity
28. Valid Universal Principles
29. God's Spirit and Truth
30. Man Made in God's Image
31. Purpose of Human Life
32. Universal Biblical Truths
33. The Bible and Human Nature
34. Biblical Salvation Knowledge
35. The Spiritual Domain
36. Cultural Transformation
37. Kingdom of Righteousness
38. The Nature of Love
39. The Gift of Life
40. The Gift of Jesus Christ
41. The Household of Faith
42. Universal Christian Values
43. The Armor of God
44. Transcending Power
45. God's Ultimate Authority
46. God's Sovereign Jurisdiction
47. New Creature in Christ
48. Salvation in Jesus Christ

The above-enumerated goals and themes apply to all humanity on earth. They represent the love of God for humanity and the gift of God to save humanity God offers these goals and themes to partner with mankind to enlighten humanity; to enrich, sustain, enhance and show the way to eternal salvation through Jesus Christ.

THE BIBLE IS THE ULTIMATE UNIVERSAL AUTHORITY ON HUMAN LIFE AND HEALTH THE BIBLE IS INCLUSIVE OF ALL VALUES ESSENTIAL FOR MANKIND'S SALVATION THE BIBLE HAS THE MESSAGE TO TRANSFORM HUMAN INSTITUTIONS

The Bible's Transforming Power

1. The Bible Transforms Minds, Hearts and Spirits.
2. The Bible Transforms the Lives of Men, Women and Children.
3. The Bible Transforms Lives, Social Relationships and Families.
4. The Bible Transforms Educational, Ideological and Spiritual Institutions.
5. The Bible Transforms Religious and Philosophical Institutions.
6. The Bible Transforms Governmental and Political Institutions.
7. The Bible Transforms Economic and Business Enterprises.
8. The Bible Transforms Cities, States and Nations.
9. The Bible Transforms Cultures, Cults and Corruption.

10. The Bible Transforms the Degeneration of Civilizations.
11. The Bible Transforms the Ethics and Morals of Humanity.
12. The Bible Transforms the Secular Cities of Men to the Sacred Kingdom of God.

FOUR THOUSAND-PLUS YEARS OF HISTORY HAVE CONFIRMED THE VALIDITY OF THE TRANSFORMING POWER OF GOD'S BIBLICAL WORD. HUMANITY AND CIVILIZATION ARE AT A DANGEROUS JUNCTURE IN THE TWENTY-FIRST CENTURY THAT REQUIRES THE TRANSFORMING POWER OF GOD'S WORD. THEREFORE, ALL OF AMERICA'S RELIGIOUS, EDUCATIONAL, POLITICAL, ECONOMIC AND SOCIAL INSTITUTIONS MUST BEGIN TO PRIORITIZE THE TEACHING, PREACHING, WITNESSING AND DISSEMINATING OF GOD'S BIBLICAL WORD IN THE CULTURE OF AMERICA AS NEVER BEFORE. THE CHURCH, AMERICANS AND THE BELIEVERS IN THE BIBLE AND JESUS CHRIST CAN NO LONGER IGNORE THE TRUTH OF THE WORD OF GOD.

"HOW SHALL WE ESCAPE, IF WE NEGLECT SO GREAT SALVATION?' (Hebrews 2:3)
The Christian Institute of Public Theology

AN URGENT CALL TO ALL LEADERS AND HUMANITY THE SUMMONS AND METHOD TO SAVE CIVILIZATION AND HUMANITY THROUGH TEACHING THE BIBLICAL WORD OF GOD TO ALL PEOPLE

-THE CHOICE: ACCEPT GOD'S WORD OR PERISH-

God's Exclusive Biblical Word Offers Mankind the Following KNOWLEDGE:

1. The knowledge of God and God's creation.
2. The knowledge of God's relationship to mankind.
3. The knowledge for life and living.
4. Knowledge for the purpose of life for all mankind.
5. Knowledge of the WILL OF GOD and PROPHECY.
6. Knowledge of God's Natural Laws.
7. Knowledge of God's Divine Governing Laws a Commandments.
8. Knowledge of God's Absolute Authority and Sovereignty.
9. Knowledge of Human Nature and Man's Rebellious Nature.
10. Knowledge of God's Sacrificial Redemption for Mankind.
11. Knowledge of God's Salvation Plan for Mankind.
12. God's Revelation of Eternal Life in JESUS CHRIST for MANKIND.

THE BIBLE REVEALS GOD'S AGONIZING LOVE AND CONCERN FOR MANKIND. GOD CREATED MAN IN HIS IMAGE AND LIKENESS. GOD GIVES MAN THE

AUTONOMY AND FREEDOM TO CHOOSE. GOD SHOWS MAN WHAT IS TRUE, GOOD, JUST, RIGHTEOUS AND BEAUTIFUL. GOD REVEALS TO MAN HIS WILL, WAYS AND WISDOM IN THE BIBLE, IN. THE HISTORY OF ISRAEL AND IN THE BIRTH, LIFE, TEACHINGS, CRUCIFIXION, RESURRECTION AND ASCENSION OF JESUS CHRIST. IGNORANCE, WICKEDNESS AND EVIL IN CONJUNCTION WITH THE POTENTIAL DESTRUCTIVENES OF TECHNOLOGY CREATE AN URGENCY TO BEGIN IMMEDIATELY TO TEACH BIBLICAL KNOWLEDGE TO ALL HUMANITY, BEGINNING WITH OUR CHILDREN. TODAY IS THE DAY OF SALVATION!!!

A CIVILIZED GOVERNMENT PROTECTS INALIENABLE HUMAN RIGHTS
SOCIAL JUSTICE IS THE DUTY OF A DEMOCRATIC GOVERNMENT

The government protection of the inalienable God-given human rights fosters the optimum actualization of the God-given human potential to achieve and experience the following blessings of God to:

1. Embrace the reality of truth.
2. Seek the life giving and enlightenment of knowledge.
3. Experience the balance and congruence of justice.
4. Appreciate and extol the virtues of goodness.
5. Follow the ways of righteousness.
6. Embrace and savor the preciousness and value of love.
7. Enjoy and behold the esthetic beauty of artistic expressions.
8. See and visualize the illumination of light and enlightenment.
9. Wait with patience for the resilience of hope.
10. Hold on and hold out with the perseverance of faith.
11. Realize the gift and understanding of wisdom.
12. Use wisely and gratefully the autonomy of freedom.

THE LOVING GOD OF LOVE HAS ENDOWED MANKIND WITH UNLIMITED AND INEXHAUSTIBLE POTENTIAL FOR THE GOOD LIFE, THE ABUNDANT LIFE AND EVEN ETERNAL LIFE. IT IS WRITTEN AND CONFIRMED IN THE BIBLICAL WORD OF GOD! Governments are instituted to protect these inalienable rights from God!

(The Christian Institute of Public Theology)

INITIATIVES TO PROTECT AND PROSPER HUMAN LIFE
Enumerations to Sustain Human Survival Values
The Christian Institute of Public Theology

1. Initiatives to Promote Healthy Relationships and Marriages
2. Initiatives to Promote Healthy Parental Childcare
3. Initiatives to Protect the Divine Human Rights of the Unborn
4. Initiatives to Educate Parents for Child Rearing and Development
5. Initiatives for Healthy Youth Growth and Development
6. Initiatives to Protect the Wellbeing of Children and Youth
7. Initiatives to Promote comprehensive Protection of Children and Youth
8. Initiatives to Provide Guidance for Optimum Education for Children & Youth
9. Initiatives to Properly Train and Educate Children and Youth
10. Initiatives for Providing and Maintaining Healthy living and Growth
11. Initiatives to Provide Character Education and Healthy Social
1. Interactions
12. Initiatives to Teach the Spiritual Domain of Learning
13. Initiatives for Assuring Validated True Education
14. Initiatives to Promote Biblical Knowledge and Spiritual Values

15. Initiatives to Instill and Safeguard Human Survival Values
16. Initiatives for Optimum Educational Achievement & Talent Development
17. Initiatives for Advanced Civilized Refinement and Development
18. Initiatives for Cultural Enrichment and Integrity Attainment
19. Initiatives for the Attainment of Human Civility, Dignity, Respect and Love
20. Initiatives to Teach Sound Doctrines, Biblical Knowledge, Wisdom and Truth
21. Initiatives to promote the Goodwill of Mankind and the Righteousness of God
22. Initiatives to Identify and Major in the Priorities of Human Life
23. Initiatives for the Establishment of Public Official Leadership Competency
24. Initiatives for Professional Certification and Ethical Competency for Public Office
25. Initiatives to Establish and Maintain Merit Systems for Public Office & Leadership
26. Initiatives to Disallow Serving in Public Office where there are Conflicts of Interest
27. Initiatives to Extinguish Injustice, Hatred, Ignorance, Incompetence & Evil from Society
28. Initiatives to Acknowledge God in private & Public as A Nation Under God
29. Initiatives for Prioritizing Biblical Education in All Institutions of Learning
30. Initiatives to Require Biblical Education as History & Literature in All Institutions
31. Initiatives to Incorporate Biblical knowledge in

All Health & Educational Facilities
32. Initiatives to Incorporate Biblical/Theological knowledge in Healthcare Services
33. Initiatives to promote Goodwill for the Common Good of All Humanity
34. Initiatives to Promote Biblical/Ethical/Theological Values for All Humanity.

THESE INITIATIVES HAVE THE POTENTIAL TO MAXIMIZE THE HUMAN POTENTIAL AND THE BLESSINGS OF GOD UPON ALL PEOPLE AND ALL NATIONS. LET US BEGIN NOW TO TAKE THESE INITIATIVES FOR THE NEW HEAVEN AND THE NEW EARTH PROMISED BY GOD THROUGH THE SAVIOR, JESUS CHRIST!!!

AMERICANS' RIGHT FOR COMPETENT REPRESENTATION
Competent Leadership has been Neglected
Christian Institute of Public Theology

The right to vote must be balanced by the right to competent leadership and democratic representation. The political advocacy for the right to vote gives substantial news, promotion and legislation. Voting rights and associated issues such as alleged suppression of voting, the handling of ballots, proper personal identification and other prerequisites for voting are prevalent topics in the news media. However, the preoccupation with voting rights and associated concerns have totally neglected and ignored the complementary essential and even vital rights for competent elected officials, competent leaders and competent democratic representatives. Hardly any credible, valid, relevant or meritorious requirements are stipulated for the candidates for public office. There is more concern about the diversity of the candidates for public office than there is about merit and fitness for the responsibilities and duties of the respective public office.

The lack of specified basic requirements for public office works against the U.S. Constitution, democracy, America and common sense. The American electoral process and requirements have not kept pace with cultural changes, global connections and technological advances. The American standards for competent and effective political administration and leadership Do not measure up to the new escalating demanding complexities of the heterogeneous globalized Twenty-First Century. Incompetent leadership and undemocratic leadership nullify and even defeat the noble purpose and reasons for voting. Voting in a democratic form of government is intended to assure the best representation of the collective will of the citizens based on their guiding constitution and values of justice, freedom and equality for the common good of the society, nation and humanity.

The social processes of immigration, acculturation, socialization and assimilation of a variety of populations of people extend far beyond their race, skin color, language, accents and customs. Human beings also have belief systems, ideologies and social values that influence their thinking, values and behaviors. Many of these ideologies, nationalities and belief systems are incompatible, irreconcilable and even conflicting. The conglomeration of these social, political and cultural values must be acknowledged in a heterogeneous society such as America which has been known as a melting pot. Many values that people adhere to are not easily assimilated. These differences must be acknowledged and reconciled with the established guiding principles, values and laws of America. There is great space for freedom and differences of ideas and opinions. However, the legally and officially established standards must prevail in the leadership of the American Government. These values and guiding principles of the Nation must be taught and embraced, especially by the American Government's political leadership and political representatives.

It is true that America is a country of immigrants with people of diverse backgrounds from all around the earth. Traditionally, immigrants came to America and were willing to assimilate, embrace American values, and democracy and become full-fledged Americans. That trend has changed. Many people who migrate to America desire to hold on to the values, political systems, ethnicities and cultures of their native countries. Many of these different newcomers to America do not embrace America's democracy, its Constitution, social values or the Judeo-Christian faith. Some of the newcomers and those who come to study in the universities and for other reasons prefer making changes in the American Government and the American society as well. During this Twenty-First Century in America, great emphasis is placed on diversity. Political identities are rampant in America. The emphasis being placed on identities, especially, race, gender, LGBT, democrat, republican, independent, conservative, liberal and so forth, are precipitating significant division in America. These differences are pervading education from kindergarten through the universities. These identities are being used for political influence. Substantial indoctrination is taking place. Political leadership and other institutional leadership are challenged. Therefore, it will require more than voting or even integrity in voting to cultivate the quality of enlightened leadership that is needed.

The guiding doctrines and principles have served America well. They have brought about great social and political reform in America. They have propelled America to be the greatest nation known to history in providing individual liberty, prosperity and national political power. These values are still sound. They have already withstood the test of time. These values and guiding principles must be taught more thoroughly and deliberately. America just keeps its identity as ONE NATION UNDER GOD. INDIVIDUAL FREEDOMS IN THE AMERICAN GOVERNMENT MUST BE SUBJECTED TO AND GUIDED BY THE CONSTITUTION OF THE UNITED STATES. THE DECLARATION OF INDEPENDENCE, PLEDGE OF ALLEGIANCE, HOLD ONTO IN GOD WE TRUST, THE TRADITIONAL BIBLICAL

VALUES THAT UNDERGIRD AND SUPPORT A DEMOCRATIC FORM OF GOVERNMENT.

To assure the true sound responsible leadership of the Democratic government from the local, state and federal levels; all candidates or public office must meet designated requirements that assure their mental and physical professional competence, their ideologies and belief systems are compatible with the U.S. Constitution, Declaration and traditional Biblical values and be otherwise fit for duty standards. The American citizens have a right to ethical, competent and representative public office holders and leaders of justice, righteousness and liberty. THIS IS AN URGENT AND IMMEDIATE PRIORITY FOR THE US CONGRESS AND THE PRESIDENCY TO ESTABLISH COMPETENT REQUIREMENTS AND STANDARDS FOR CANDIDATES FOR AMERICAN PUBLIC OFFICE FOR THE HEALTH, SAFETY, SECURITY, LIBERTY, PEACE, GOOD WILL FOR ALL AMERICANS AND THE PEOPLE OF GOD.

GUIDING PRINCIPLES FOR DEMOCRACY

U.S. Guiding Principles Offer Unity for America

America is blessed with the most noble human uniting governing principles known to mankind. America is a republic of 50 united states, embracing the Declaration of Independence proclaiming that God created equality of all poles. The Declaration of Independence proclaims the inherent endowment by the Creator of certain unalienable rights for all men (all people); among these rights are life, liberty and the pursuit of happiness. The sound doctrine of the Declaration of Independence is a guiding principle for the unity of the United States and for all the citizens and people of America.

The founders and architects of the creeds to govern the United States formulated a noble idea for governing the United States. This noble idea was a democratic form of government. A democratic form of government insures a government by the people, for the people and of the people. This noble idea of democracy evolved and resulted in the written document of the Constitution of the United States of America, along with a Bill of Rights. The Constitution of the United States of America, and the Bill of Rights, confirm that America is covenanted to be governed by the Law and not by men.

The governing and guiding principles of the Declaration of Independence and The Constitution of the United States of America were founded upon Biblical Judeo-Christian principles. It is historically documented that the men who wrote the Declaration of Independence and, The U.S Constitution of America were Christian Believers. Additionally, a large number, of these men were theologically trained. Christianity is inclusive of all humanity. It does not force itself upon anyone. It is consistent with God's gift of autonomy to each individual to choose. No one is forced or can be forced to be a Christian or to accept Jesus Christ as Lord and Savior. It is the individual's autonomous choice.

It is well documented in American Church history along with names, places and dates that Christianity was spread throughout the thirteen colonies, beginning in 1607. American Church history records The Great Awakening in America in 1726. This Great Awakening consisted of massive proclamations, exhortations, teaching, preaching revivals, conversions and spreading the Gospel of Jesus Christ. This Great Awakening accelerated the American culture with biblical study. Christian beliefs and doctrines.

This seeding of Christianity in the American culture in the sixteenth and seventeenth centuries were precursor and foundational for the Declaration of Independence in 1776 and the signing of the Constitution on September 17, 1787. This is suggestive that the founders of America's guiding governing democratic documents were based on available ethical, just, legal and theological, sound moral doctrines and principles. These governing documents were derived from a rich, knowledgeable, ethical, social and spiritual American culture.

These true time-tested guiding universal principles, equitable laws, ethical values and God-inspired human spirits transformed America into the most prosperous, powerful and blessed nation of earth. America is considered an exceptional nation because it acknowledges itself as, "One nation under God, with liberty and justice for all, " and the "evidentiary truths that all men are created equal, and are endowed by the Creator with certain "unalienable rights among them, life, liberty and the pursuit of happiness."

Serious problems have been detected regarding the maintenance and continuation of America as an exceptional nation under God. Can America neglect or stray away from its guiding principles and remain an exceptional nation under God? Many American problems could be analyzed, to explore answers to this question. The last two decades have produced problems in the general political election process. The voting process in recent years has caused massive confusion, litigation, bitterness and debate.

There are two faulty presumptions in the American political election process. The first presumption encourages the optimum utilization of voting to have a successful democratic government. However, voting alone does not assure a successful democracy. Incompetent and unfit candidates can and often are voted into office. Candidates who do not believe in democracy can be overwhelmingly elected to public office. The emphasis and priority on the encouragement to vote is not sufficient to maintain and sustain American democracy. The second faulty presumption in the political election process is that the majority makes the best choice for the people and the nation. However, majority numbers do not always translate into ethical or best decisions and choices for the people or the nation. It is clear and logically concluded that a majority can be against the guiding principles of a democratic government.

This brief discourse on Guiding Principles for Democracy makes it clear chat a true and effective democratic form of government requires specified true knowledge, comprehensive education, professional competence, sound philosophical ideologies, ethical and moral standards congruent with sound biblical doctrines and the benevolent spiritual compassion of Jesus Christ.

In order to maintain and sustain the indispensable vitally needed democratic form of government, America must begin now to revolutionize its public educational systems with required Biblical Education as History and Literature, Character Education, Ethical and Moral Education, Health Education, Legal Education, Artistic Education, Marriage and Family Education, Vocational Education, Patriotic Education, Theological Education, Liberal Arts Education, Technological Education, Science Education, Engineering Education, Sanctity of Life Education, Religions Liberty, Human Individual Freedom Education for Civilized Living.

The above educational curriculum, truths, knowledge standards and values have been tested and validated by ancient of times, and universal civilizations have proved to be the highest merits of civilized living. Therefore, to forfeit or to deviate from these time-tested and validated guiding principles for democracy is tantamount to disavowing civilization, cursing mankind and declaring open rebellion against the Creator God.

What has happened to American Democracy in this 21st Century? Why is there so much confusion, so many conflicts and divisiveness in the United States? In my book, The Way Out of Darkness, some foundations for the American Culture Crisis are addressed. Here, a very brief synopsis is provided. In the early years of American history from the 17th to the early 20th Century, millions of immigrants came to America with multiple nationalities, races, ethnicities, religions and cultural backgrounds. However, these immigrants with their multiple cultural backgrounds assimilated into the American Culture and became identified as Americans. Most of them assimilated, accepted or were influenced by the predominant Judea-Christian faith and values of the American Democracy. The doctrines, of the Judeo-Christian faith, makes possible a human assimilation and acculturation of differences into a great and glorious harmonious heterogeneous oneness. It allows human beings to maintain their unique God-given ethnicities and differences, and still be civil and benevolent brothers and sisters. The Biblical Word says," There is neither Jew nor Greek, there is neither bond nor free, there is neither male nor female: for you are all one in Christ Jesus (Galatians 3:28).

Those guiding Biblical, Declaration of Independence and One Nation under God principles sown into the American Culture, brought America through the Civil War and reunited the North and South. These guiding principles emancipated the Negro American slaves. These biblical-based democratic principles through the leadership of Dr. Martin Luther King, Jr. brought about the greatest nonviolent social revolution in world history in America.

America is blessed with God-inspired and directed guiding principles of democracy that are inclusive of all people of goodwill. These standards of governance for mankind are set and authorized by God. The time-tested and validated guiding principles for the United States of America are: THE BIBLE, THE DECLARATION OF INDEPENDENCE, THE CONSTITUTION OF THE UNITED STATES OF AMERICA, THE PLEDGE OF ALLEGIANCE TO THE FLAG AND THE REPUBLIC FOR WHICH IT STANDS, AS ONE NATION UNDER GOD, INDIVISIBLE, WITH LIBERTY AND JUSTICE FOR ALL, and THE **MOTTO**: IN GOD WE TRUST (not man). These are the God INSPIRED INFALLIBLE PRINCIPLES TO LEAD AND GUIDE AMERICA AND ALL

GOD'S PEOPLE ACCORDING TO THE DEMOCRATIC FORM OF GOVERNMENT.

These guiding principles are consistent with the echoing spirits of two great American Presidents. President Dwight D. Eisenhower stated, "America is great because she is good. If she ceases to be good, she will cease to be great." President John F. Kennedy exclaimed, "Ask not what your country can do for you, ask what you can do for your country."

AMERICAN CITIZENS FOR DEMOCRACY

AMERICAN COALITION

AMERICA'S VITAL GUIDING PRINCIPLES
Prerequisites for Effective Leadership
The Christian Institute of Public Theology

The guiding and leadership principles of America are established by specific laws, certain truths, traditions and documents. The U.S. Constitution contains the specific laws. The Declaration of Independence contains certain specific truths. The United States Pledge of Allegiance as One Nation under God and its motto, "In God we Trust," contain the mandates, values and traditions. The Holy Bible is the universal foundational document for all of America's governing laws, ethical values and guiding principles.

The American guiding and leadership principles incorporate a long list of specific ideas and values (along with their enumerated antitheses, which must be defeated). These following specific universal ideas and values are not random, arbitrary or frivolous. The enumerated ideas and values are congruent with God's revelation of truth contained in the Holy Bible and in the life and Gospel of Jesus Christ. Jesus is at the center of history that creates a point in time that designates the backward count before Jesus Christ came, and the forward count after he came into the world and history. B.C. is the backward count to the past. It means Before Christ. A. D. is the abbreviation for the Latin word, Anno domini, which means "In the Year of Our Lord." It is the forward count from the birth of Christ. The Bible has a genealogy in the Book of Matthews (Matthews 1:1-17) of Jesus Christ that counts backward from the birth of Christ back to David and Abraham. The Book of Luke records the genealogy of Jesus

Christ from Christ back to David, Abraham, Adam and God (Luke 3:23-38). The current date of this writing is 10/28/2021 AD, In the year of our Lord. Christ was born on the earth Two Thousand Twenty-One years ago. Each time a date is made or referenced in world history, it is the acknowledgment of the BIRTH AND COMING OF JESUS CHRIST.

In as much as Jesus is proclaimed as Lord of Lords, King of Kings and the Prince of Peace; why not learn about the noble governing and guiding principles of Jesus Christ? Why attempt to deny the best-known and most celebrated and exalted person of history? Why ignore the best-known and the most universally validated book of history? It is the ultimate book of law, history, truth and guiding principles of government and human life The deaf ears, deceptive minds, hateful hearts and evil spirits of the world do not qualify to be in any leadership or public policy-making position in the American Government. Only those persons with the competence, compassion and commitment to be guided by the established laws, Biblical Principles and survival values should be considered for American Government leadership or any human leadership position of GOD'S PEOPLE.

JESUS CHRIST IS THE ULTIMATE PROLIFE, ABUNDANT LIFE, ETERNAL LIFE, ALL TIME LEADER. HIS LIFE AND MINISTRY INCORPORATE ALL THE PRINCIPLES AND VALUES FOR LEADERSHIP. GOD HAS PROVIDED SPECIFIC IDEAS, LAWS, PRINCIPLES AND VALUES CONGRUENT WITH THE VALIDATED TRUTH OF SCIENCE, ART, LAW, THEOLOGY AND CHRIST, TO DEFEAT EVIL AND SPIRITUAL WICKEDNESS IN THE RAGING WARFARE AGAINST HUMAN SURVIVAL VALUES.

THE SPIRITUAL AND CULTURAL BATTLEFIELD

The Warfare Against Survival Values

SURVIVAL VALUES		DESTRUCTIVE CHOICES
Goodness	VS	Evil
Truth	VS	Lies
Love	VS	Hatred
Justice	VS	Injustice
Knowledge	VS	Ignorance
Wisdom	VS	Foolishness
Understanding	VS	Confusion
Hope	VS	Despair
Faith	VS	Doubt
Godliness	VS	Idolatry
Reason	VS	Irrationality
Mercy	VS	Cruelty
Order	VS	Chaos
Peace	VS	War
Sacred	VS	Secular
Enlightenment	VS	Cognitive Deficiency
Righteousness	VS	Wrongful
Wholeness	VS	Divisive
Civility	VS	Barbarianism
Purity	VS	Corruption
Beauty	VS	Offensive
Charitable	VS	Self-Centered
Innocent	VS	Guilty
Positive	VS	Negativity

Humility	VS	Arrogance
Secure	VS	Endangered
Progressive	VS	Regressive
Goodwill	VS	Envious
Refinement	VS	Crude
Joyful	VS	Miserable
Inspiration	VS	Demoralization
Generosity	VS	Greed
Sacrificial Service	VS	Fraudulent Exploitation
Benevolence	VS	Malevolence
Altruistic	VS	Jealousy
Restoration	VS	Destruction
Elevate	VS	Denigrate
Freedom	VS	Bondage
Salvation	VS	Damnation
Life	VS	Death

The above enumerations of SURVIVAL VALUES and the opposite DESTRUCTIVE CHOICES can be clearly separated and distinguished. The human attitudes, values and behaviors of these survival values and destructive choices can be determined through a variety of human actions and expressions. These clear choices make possible wise and intelligent decisions. The loving God created man and woman in his image with the autonomous ability to make decisions based on God's knowledge, truth and wisdom. God created a dichotomy of opposites to avoid confusion. He created male and female. God created light and darkness, day and night. Ie created sweet and bitter; up and down, north and south, east and west. God enables man (woman included) to make choices between survival values and disobedient destructive choices. God provides the blueprint for human survival in the Holy Bible. He sent messengers of priests, prophets, kings and angels. The Bible is a comprehensive law book containing laws, commandments, principles with true principles, ethics and values to govern and guide mankind and the nations in all walks of life. Last of all God sent Jesus Christ as the unmistakable embodiment of all the survival values. Jesus Christ is the GREAT ULTIMATE I AM OF LIFE'S SURVIVAL AND SALVATION VALUES FOR ALL MANKIND. HISTORY HAS VALIDATED THE UNIQUE TRUTH OF JESUS CHRIST.

THE SPIRITUAL AND CULTURAL WARFARE IN AMERICA AND THE WORLD IN THIS 21s CENTURY, AD, REQUIRES AND DEMANDS THE STEADFAST ADOPTION OF THE SURVIVAL VALUES AS PROVIDED BY THE LOVING GOD AND SACRIFICIAL SON, JESUS CHRIST.

The Christian Institute of Public Theology

THE RATIONALE FOR RESOLUTIONS

Proposals for Solving Problems and Elevating Humanity

-The Public Theologian-

The initiatives of salvation resolutions for cultural transformation are based on the words of Jesus, "And I say unto you, ask, and it shall be given you; seek, and ye shall find; knock, and it shall be opened unto you (Luke 11:9)." It is essential to make real the appeals to the appropriate persons, representatives and authorities. There is a need to be explicit in your request and what you want. The heart of your resolution appeal must be based on truth, righteousness, justice and the validated word of God for the public good.

The resolutions are written proposals and appeals for responsive action. In order to get things done, some form of action is required. Faith without works is dead. Cursing the darkness is not productive. Negative moaning, groaning and complaining rarely accomplish anything of significance. Hatred and ill will against perceived enemies are not redemptive for cultural transformation. The resolution proposal and appeal not only make a formal request, but it makes known the just, righteous and humanitarian beneficial resolution to the issue or problem at hand. It is empowered by the grace and the congruence of God's Will.

The well-planned and written resolution explains the existing problematic concerns and the means and methods of resolving the problematic concerns. In as much as the resolution has enumerated the problem and provided the written recommendations, proposals and solutions, the receiving authority only needs to receive, accept, adopt and implement the submitted resolution. The public theologian assures that the sound doctrine of Scripture is incorporated into the resolution.

SOME NEEDED RESOLUTIONS FOR CULTURAL TRANSFORMATION

1. Resolution for Character Education from K-12 in all Public Schools.
2. Resolution for Biblical Education from K-12 in all Public Schools.
3. Resolution for Black American History Education in all U.S. Educational Institutions.
4. Resolution for Black American Music Art in all Public Educational Institutions.
5. Resolution for Black American Restoration for Racial Enslavement & Discrimination.
6. Resolution for Government Administrative Equity & Merit Systems for all citizens.
7. Resolution for Required Bible Courses for All American Law Schools & Judges.
8. Resolution for Validated Educational, Ethical, Mental & Moral Fitness for Public Office.
9. Resolution for Establishment of Validated Professional Competent Code of Ethics.
10. Resolution for Vocational Education and Artistic Education in all Public Schools.
11. Resolution for Protective Holistic Child Care, Nurture, Education, Health & Training.

12. Resolution for Reaffirmation of Strict Observance of U.S. Constitutional Law Equitably.

THE PUBLIC THEOLOGIANS WHO ACCEPT THE WHOLE GOSPEL FOR THE WHLOE PERSON FOR THE WHLOE WORLD MUST BE RESOLUTE IN THE PURSUIT OF TRUTH, JUSTICE & SALVATION.

SALVATION RESOLUTIONS FOR THE PUBLIC GOOD
Resolutions for Cultural Transformation
-The Public Theologian-

Resolution for Character Education	
Resolution for Ethical Education	
Resolution for Biblical Education	
Resolution for Artistic Education	
Resolution for Vocational Education	
Resolution for Theological Education	
Resolution for Administrative Merit System	
Resolution for U.S Constitution Education	
Resolution for Declaration of Independent Education	
Resolution for Pledge of Allegiance to U.S. Flag	
Resolution for Gender Education and Roles	
Resolution for Religion Pluralism Education	
Resolution for Cultural Diversity Education and Competence	
Resolution for Church and State Synchronization	
Resolution for Human Heterogeneous Cooperation	
Resolution for Nations Under God	
Resolution for Democratic Government	

Resolution for Child Care and Child Rearing	
Resolution for Courtship and Marriage	
Resolution for Transmission of Moral Values	
Resolution for Assimilation of Christian Values	
Resolution for Public Office Qualification	
Resolution for Maintaining Quality Public Schools	
Resolution for the Unique University of the Bible	

It is recommended that a thorough one-page resolution be written of each of the resolutions above to be presented, submitted and transmitted to appropriate representatives, pastors, ministers, churches, and educational and governmental institutions. These resolutions are written to become public policy, ordinances, legislation and laws. These resolutions are to be studied, discussed in various groups, and classes and incorporated into educational curricula in all educational institutions from the public schools through the university systems of higher learning. The basic universal truths contained in these resolutions must be incorporated in the established American institutions of family, church, school, business and government in order to affect the vitally needed cultural transformation in the American society. These resolutions are designed for urgent positive implementation of actions and change for the gift of humanity.

THE MERITS OF PUBLIC EDUCATION HAS BEEN VALIDATED

The American Public-School Systems and public education have served America very well. Public education, even during the racial segregation period (Prior to Brown vs Board of Education, May 17, 1954), served Black Americans very well. The most renowned Black American leaders and educators attended predominantly Black American public schools. The education of Black American children in segregated public schools is a significant story worthy of revisiting and exploring within itself. American public education in conjunction with compulsory school education laws has earned the merit of being the most effective method of educating the masses of American children and incorporating democratic values in the process. American Public education has a history of incorporating along with the academics, moral, ethical, spiritual and patriotic values undergirded by Judea-Christian Biblical values.

THE ATTACK UPON PUBLIC EDUCATION:

This proven meritorious public education system has come under serious attack with a predictable trajectory of educational regression and destruction of moral, ethical and democratic values. Tragically, this detrimental attack is being initiated by an illegal and undemocratic process of transferring public funds along with administrative authority to autonomously and independently operated privatized, "Charter Schools" with no direct accountability to the public taxpaying citizens. It is a blatant violation of

"Taxation without Representation." These charter schools have built-in administrative arbitrary, flexible standards, policies and procedures that insidiously and illegally exempt the charter school officials from U.S. Constitutional Law, Human Rights violations, Civil Rights violations, ethical codes and government professional standards.

The Charter School Choice Movement is the most detrimental educational initiative in U.S. History. It authorizes the solicitation of public and private funding to operate privatized charter schools for profit with arbitrary flexible standards and without administrative accountability to the public. The Charter School Choice Movement is deteriorating the public education system into a for-profit educational predatory industrial complex at the expense of public education and quality in education for the public.

THE ATTACK UPON PUBLIC EDUCATION

This uninformed and ill-conceived educational initiative with no moral, ethical, lawful and professional compass or standards represents a "Pandora's Box of degenerative confusion, corruption, evil, divisiveness and destruction. These terms are extreme, but they are true, serious and lethal. The Charter School Choice initiatives accentuate and specialize in class, racial, ethnic and hetero generous differences instead of human and American homogeneous commonalities for the common good of society. The charter school choice attack on public education is an attack on the core values of America and its primary institutions. It is a blind movement totally uninformed and shortsighted.

RECOMMENDATION:

This unprecedented (knowingly or unknowingly) attack upon public education must be challenged at every legitimate ethical, moral, scientific, artistic and legal domain to the highest appeals of government, the people and to God. This public education attack transcends education. IT JEOPARDIZES THE NATION!

The Christian Association of Public Theologians, Inc. Atlanta, GA.

COURAGEOUS STANDARDS FOR AMERICAN LEADERSHIP
Human Leadership Standards Must be True, Just and Righteous

America must prioritize competence and qualifications for public and political office consistent with democratic values, the United States Constitution, the Declaration of Independence and the biblical foundational creeds as a Nation under God. The National self-interest and the security of America require adherence to the Nation's ethical, Constitutional values, moral, social and civil humanitarian standards.

CORE STANDARDS FOR LEADERSHIP

1. The Biblical and Historical validated righteousness of God.
2. Biblical validated Truth of the Unique Holy Bible.
3. Validated competent just leadership representation.
4. Representation for the common good of humanity.
5. Human justice, righteousness and truth leadership.
6. Adherence to Sound doctrines and validated ethical values.
7. Professional competence of science, art, law and theology.
8. Pro-human life reverence in all human representative services.
9. Guided by excellence in all qualitative products and services.
10. Respect for autonomous human freedom and rights endowed by God.

11. Observance of the equitable acquisition and allocation of God's gifts.
12. Faithful stewardship of God's gift of life and infinite resources.

AMERICA MUST BEGIN NOW TO ESTABLISH, REQUIRE AND ASSIMILATE THESE CORE SURVIVAL VALUES AND STANDARDS FOR ALL PEOPLE WITHIN THE JURISDICTION OF AMERICA. THESE VALUES CAN BE SUSTAINED THROUGH THE FOLLOWING EDUCATION: Biblical Education, Declaration of Independence, Theological Education, Patriotic Education, Constitution of United States, Christian Education, Moral & Ethical Education, Liberal Arts Education, Character Education, Democratic Government Education, American History Including Black American History, World History, Vocational Education, Free Enterprise System, Science, Art, Law and Theology. THIS EDUCATIONAL CURRICULUM ENCOMPASSES THE MOST NOBLE AND ADVANCED KNOWLEDGE KNOWN TO MANKIND.

-KNOWLEDGE TO KEEP HUMANITY FROM PERISHING-

THEOLOGICAL LEADERSHIP IMPERATIVES
Prerequisites for Effective Leadership
The Christian Institute of Public Theology

FOUNDATIONS FOR LEADERSHIP

1. Know the Truth. Learn Relevant Knowledge. Be Wise, Reasonable, Rational, understanding, and Focused.
2. Embrace Truth, Justice, Goodness, Beauty, Hope and Mercy.
3. Follow Pathways of Righteousness and the Light of Enlightenment.
4. Obey God. Oppose Evil, Hatred and Wickedness.

LEADERSHIP REQUIREMENTS

1. Obedience to the Divine Imperatives: COME, TARRY AND GO: Come to yourself, Come to Jesus. Tarry for the Education, Regeneration, Identification, Mission and Empowerment. G.O. to your own people with the Gospel. Go to other people with this Gospel. Go to the whole world with this Gospel.

2. Education and training program of Certified, Degreed, Licensed, Ordained Intellectual Competence. This is a part of the whole armor of God that is required.

3. The Optimum Scientific, Artistic, Legalistic and Theistic Educational Achievement of Recognized Bodies of Knowledge and Educational Institutions.

4. Endowed with a Solid Moral Character of Human Dignity, Reverence and Integrity Based on A Specific Belief System that is rooted in Biblical Authority and Established by God.

5. Educated through a Qualified Certification of Biblical Literacy and Knowledge-based Competent Documented Study.

6. The Endowment of the New Birth and the New Creature in Jesus Christ following the Admonition of Jesus to Nicodemus: "You Must be Born Again." You must be able to Discern and Engage in the Spiritual Domain of God.

7. Endowed with the ability to Discern Spirits whether they be of God. Must be able to Discern False Spirits and False Prophets and Anti-Christ Spirits. Jesus admonished his Disciples to be Wise as Serpents. Know the God Spirit that Confesses that Jesus has Come in the Flesh.

8. Must be Grounded in Universal Principles of Love, Goodness, Equality, Freedom, Justice, Hope and Faith; and not be Captivated by Cultism, Sectarianism, Racism, Partisan Divisions, Genderism and other Divisive ISMS. Embrace Universal Values and Principles.

9. Must understand the Skills to Disclose: COST-BENEFIT ANALISIS, VALUES CLARIFICATION, CONFLICT RESOLUTION, SUCCESS IDENTITY,

FUTURE ORIENTATION FOCUS, MENTAL STATE AND STATUS ORIENTATION.

10. THE POSITIVE TRANSFORMATION OF HATRED, RAGE AND ANGER INTO USEFUL SERVICES AND CONTRIBUTIONS. UTILIZE THE ENERGY OF RAGE FOR USEFUL WORK AND OTHER POSITIVE FOCUS.

11. CREATE A TRANSITION FROM WHAT IS TO WHAT OUGHT TO BE ACCORDING TO THE BIBLICAL STANDARDS OF GOD. FROM DOUBT TO FAITH, FROM HATE TO LOVE....

12. INSTILL A SIGNIFICANT PURPOSE IN LIFE WORTHY OF ABONDONING ALL TO FOLLOW. ADD TO THIS PURPOSE THE SIGNIFICANT BEING CREATED IN THE IMAGE OF GOD.

The Christian Institute of Public Theology

CHAPTER 12
THE MISSION OF THE GOSPEL

1. Feed and Nurture: John 21:15-17; Matthew 25:31-46

2. Love & Evangelize: John 13:34, 4:16; Mark 12:30-31; 1Cor. 13

3. Teach, Preach & Witness: Matthew 28:19; Mark 16:15

4. Heal & Restore: Luke 4:18-19; John 11:25

5. Liberate & Elevate: Luke 4:18-19; 1John 4: 1-2; John 8:32

6. Build & Establish: Matthew 6:33, Matthew 16:18; Rev. 11:15

7. Comfort & Encourage: John 14:16-18; Matthew 5:1-12

8. Warn && Prophesy: Ezekiel 3:17-21; Amos 4:12; Mathew 3:3; Col 1:28

9. Defend & Comfort: Psalm 82:3-4; Matthew 18:8-9; Ephesians 6: 11-17

10. Have Dominion: Genesis 1:28; Matthew 24:14; Romans 13:1

11. Witness Truth & Light: Matthew 5:16, 33; John 14:6

12. Follow Jesus Christ: John 14:6; Acts 4:12; Isaiah 45:23; Phil 2:9-11

There is a place and a duty for all believers in Jesus Christ to participate in the mission and ministry of Jesus Christ in whatever position or calling you may be involved regardless to your title. There is plenty room in the Kingdom of God as Expressed in (Matthew 9:37-38) and (Luke 10:2). The harvest is great and the laborers are few.

The Christian Institute of Public Theology, Inc.
Atlanta, Georgia

INITIATIVES FOR RESTORING CULTURAL VALUES
Teach and Practice the Governing Creeds of America

(The governing creeds of America include the Bible, Declaration of Independence, U.S. Constitution, Pledge of Allegiance to One Nation Under God, In God We Trust and Government of the people, for the people and by the people.)

The public theologians must take the initiative to facilitate the practice and the process of helping all American citizens to live up to the governing creeds of America in order to achieve the God-given human rights of life, liberty, pursuit of happiness, equal justice and equal protection of the laws enumerated in the Bible, American Creeds and the U.S. Constitution.

All Americans must be taught that A Nation Under God requires all citizens to be taught and learn about the knowledge and truth of God in the Holy Bible and the governing creeds of America.

RECOMMENDED INITIATIVES FOR PUBLIC THEOLOGIANS

1. Organize An Expansive Public Theology Membership Drive.
2. Publish and Distribute a Periodic Public Theologian News Letter.
3. Establish A School to Teach Public Theology. (The Institute of Public Theology).
4. Educate and Train Public Theologians as Professionals and Skilled Helpers.

5. Teach Theological Ethics. Foundations for Ethical Leadership and Professionalism.
6. Teach Values for Ethical Leadership and Business Professionalism.
7. Teach Values and Traits for Character Education.
8. Teach Public Theology and Public Policy Formulation.
9. Teach Ethical Values for Theological Leadership.
10. Teach God's Purpose and Salvation Plan for Mankind.
11. God's Way, Truth, Life and Favor for Mankind.
12. God's Will, Kingdom, Household of Faith on Earth and In Heaven.

RECOMMENDATIONS FOR THE PUBLIC GOOD:

1. Adopt Merit Systems as opposed to "Buddy Systems."
2. Avoid electing unethical & biblically illiterate leaders.
3. Avoid public representatives with conflicts of interest.

Educational References:

Holy Bible, James Strong Concordance, US Constitution, Declaration of Independence, Pledge of Allegiance, US Motto (In God We Trust), The Way Out of Darkness-Vital Public Theology (W. J. Webb); A Table of Visions to Revive the Nation (W.J. Webb),

BIBLICAL GOOD NEWS FROM GOD
Willie James Webb

The Good News of the Bible undergirds, supports, balances and authorizes all other true knowledge and education for human life to live and glorify God. The Old Testament and the New Testament are Good News from God. This Gospel is for the whole person and the whole world.

This Gospel is for attentive ears, to listen and learn. It is for the mind to understand, analyze, and synthesize. It is for the eyes to see and behold. It is for the heart to feel and believe. The Gospel is for the mouth and tongue to speak it, teach it, proclaim it and sing it. The Gospel is a heavenly sound and a joyful noise.

The Gospel is for the feet to walk it; run it; dance it; transport and expand it throughout the world. The Gospel is for the arms and hands to reach out with it; embrace it; and serve humanity with it.

The Gospel is for the mind to think it; for the heart to love it; be inspired and sing it. It is for the soul to embrace it and cherish it. The Gospel is for the believer to study it, learn it, and use it for the unfinished task of God's kingdom building on the earth.

The Gospel is for the artist to paint it; to sculpt it; to write it; to chant it and to sing it with the full force of aesthetic expression. The Gospel is for the scientist to observe and practice with honesty and truth. It is for the judiciary to incorporate, legislate and mandate with justice, equity and liberty.

The Gospel is for families to be instructed by it and for children to be nurtured by it. The Gospel is for communities to become allied with it and unified by it. The Gospel is for nations and governments to be guided. blessed and ruled by its righteousness, justice and mercy. The Gospel i: for nations to overcome their alienations, separations and states of being foreigners, strangers and enemies; and become one nation and one human family in the household and kingdom of God.

Jesus Christ is the unique best Good News to come to the earth. His birth life, ministry, crucifixion, resurrection and ascension are Good News. All of his words and actions are Good News. Everything that was said about Jesu: is Good News. Everything that was done to Jesus is Good News, including; the sacrificial crucifixion. The most amazing Good News of all is recorded by Matthew, Mark and Luke, a quote from God, "This is my Beloved Son in whom I am well pleased." Good News about the Old Testament, the Nev Testament and Jesus Christ - Is GOOD NEWS FROM GOD.

BIBLICAL AND U.S. CONSTITUTIONAL GUIDES

Sound Doctrine Public Policy Preferences For A Just, Free, Healthy, Peaceful and Prosperous America

1. Pro-Human Life as Sacred from God the Creator.

2. Patriotism for America as a Nation under God.

3. Acknowledge America and all Nations as Nations under God.

4. Acknowledge the Truth of the Holy Bible as Validated by History.

5. Acknowledge the Historical Truths of Jesus Christ as Savior Sent by God.

6. Uphold the Truths of the Bible and the Laws of the U.S. Constitution.

7. Support Judicial, Equal Justice under Just Laws, God and the U.S. Constitution.

8. Support Individual and religious Liberty under God and the U.S. Constitution.

9. Acknowledge and Respect the Sacredness of Christmas, the Cross and other Validated Religious Celebrations and Historical Monumental Symbols.

10. Establish and Utilize Just Merit-Based Administrative and Judicial Systems for Fairness, Justice and Equality.

11. Respect, Support, Leach and Encourage the True, Sound, Ethical and Moral Traditional Social Values Based on Historical Precedents, Scientific Knowledge and Biblical Truth.

12. Provide the Utmost Support for Public Education as Standard Education Designed for the Public Good as Paid for by Public Funds. Accommodate Charter Schools and other Private Bono-Fide Educational Institutions with Private Funding.

13. As Mandated by Law in Georgia, Teach Comprehensive Character Education from Kindergarten through Twelfth Grade. THE SERIOUS LETHAL MORAL VIOLENT CRISIS IN AMERICA DEMANDS MAJORING IN CHARACTER EDUCATION UNDERGIRDED BY CHRISTIAN EDUCATION.

14. As Mandated by Georgia Law, TEACH THE OLD TESTAMENT AND NEW TESTAMENT AS HISTORY, LITERATURE AND BIBLICAL KNOWLEDGE. THE DESTRUCTION OF THESE CHILDREN FOR LACK OF BIBLICAL (THEOLOGICAL) KNOWLEDGE IS DESTROYING AMERICA AND THE BLESSINGS OF GOD UPON AMERICA.

15. Support Israel and Its Democracy and All God-Fearing Nations. AMERICA HAS BEEN BLESSED TO BE A BLESSING TO THE WORLD. CHRISTIANITY WAS BORN OUT OF ISRAEL (Judaism). AMERICA HAS BEEN KNOWN AS A CHRISTIAN NATION. USA IS IN THE MIDDLE OF JER(USA) LEM. THE UNITED STATES OF AMERICA HAS A CONNECTION WITH ISRAEL AND JERUSALEM. AMERICA MUST NOT FORFEIT THE BLESSINGS OF GOD!

16. Establish Appropriate Educational, Ethical, Moral, Patriotic, Professional and Otherwise Competent and Fit for duty, Responsibility and Accountability Standards for All Elective and Public Officials Who Represent the People.

The Christian Institute of Public Theology

GOD'S SPIRITUAL GUIDANCE AND BLESSINGS FOR MANKIND

1. Fear God, and keep his commandments: for this is the whole duty of man. (Eccles. 2:13)
2. Let this mind be in you which was also in Christ Jesus. (Philippians 2:5)
3. Thou shall love the Lord thy God with all thy heart, and with all soul, and with all thy Mind. (Matthew 22:37)
4. Thou shall love thy neighbor as thyself. (Matthew 22:39)
5. Be fruitful, and multiply, and replenish the earth, and subdue it: and have dominion over the fish of the sea, and over the fowl of the air, and over every living thing that moves upon the earth. (Genesis 1:28)
6. But seek ye first the kingdom of God, and his righteousness; and all these things shall be added unto you. (Matthew 6:33)
7. Except a man be born again, he cannot see the kingdom of God. Cohn 3:3). Marvel not That I said unto thee, you must be born again. (John 3:7)
8. But be ye transformed by the renewing of your mind, that ye may prove what is that Good, and acceptable, and perfect, will of God. (Romans 12:2)
9. Fight the good fight of faith, lay hold on eternal life. (1 Timothy)
10. Be strong in the grace that is in Christ Jesus. (2Timothy 2:1)

11. Preach the word; be instant in season, out of season; reprove, rebuke, exhort with all long suffering and doctrine. (2Timothy 4:2)

12. But watch thou in all things, endure afflictions, do the work of an evangelist, make full Proof of thy ministry. (2Timothy 4:5)

13. I have fought a good fight, I have finished my course, I have kept the faith. (2Tim. 4-7)

14. Son of man, I have made thee a watchman unto the house of Israel: Therefore, hear the word at my mouth, and give them warning from me. (Ezekiel 3:17)

15. Warn the wicked. (Ezekiel 3:18-19). Warn the righteous. (Ezekiel 3:20-21)

16. Therefore, let us not sleep, as do others, but let us watch and be sober. (Thessalonians 5:6)

17. Rejoice evermore. Pray without ceasing. In everything give thanks. (Thessalonians 5:16-18)

18. I press toward the mark for the prize of the high calling of God in Christ Jesus. (Philippians 3:14)

19. But let judgment run down as waters, and righteousness as a mighty stream. (Amos 5:24)

20. Draw nigh unto God, and he will draw nigh unto you. (James 4:8)

The Christian Institute of Public Theology

The following are some considerations for writing books and music for transforming the spirit of America and mankind for the highest quality of life and living for all people. We have not begun to exhaust the blessed resources of music for the healing, liberation and salvation of humankind. Musicians are challenged to purge the art of music of its corruption and bring about an urgently needed renaissance to refine and lift the spirit of humanity in the 21st Century:

1. Enriching Children's Lives through Music.
2. Core Music for Enrichment.
3. Music Education Enrichment.
4. Refining the Art of Music.
5. Music Refinement.
6. Music for Healing.
7. Music for Transformation.
8. Transformation Music.
9. Spiritual Elevation through Music.
10. Transforming Power of Music.
11. The Myriad Sounds of Music.
12. Music's Liberating Power.
13. Music: The Art for the Soul.
14. Civilizing with Music.
15. Soul Soothing Sounds.
16. Refining the Message of Sounds.
17. Arranging Salvation Sounds.
18. Crafting Sounds for Living.
19. Crafting Sounds for Enlightenment.
20. Crafting Sounds for Reverence.
21. Crafting Sounds for Liberation.
22. Crafting Sounds for Adoration.
23. The Sounds of Love.
24. The Sounds of faith.

25. The Sounds of Hope.
26. The Sounds of Courage.
27. The Sounds of Freedom.
28. The Lyrics of God News.
29. The Lyrics of Humanity.
30. The Lyrics of Brotherhood.

The Blessings of Music (Continuation):

1. The lyrics of Hope.
2. The lyrics of God's Word.
3. Lories of Negro Spirituals.
4. Lyrics for Liberation.
5. Lyrics for Gratitude.
6. Lyrics for Praise.
7. Lyrics for Patriotism.
8. Lyrics of Christian Love.
9. Lyrics of God's Gifts.
10. Lyrics of Life Eternal.
11. The Harmony of Peace.
12. The Harmony of Goodwill.
13. The Harmony of Humanity.
14. The Harmony of Life.

This is not meant to be an exhaustive list. The sounds of music are inexhaustible in their varied forms of expression. This list is meant to show the possibility of the art of music in helping to overcome the impoverishment of human culture, the crudeness of human civility and the lost visions and hopes of the human potential. An artistic music renaissance is needed In America to revive, restore, reconstruct and give the elevated inspirational expression to the values that God gave in abundance to bless America and the world.

The human emergency and acute culture crisis in this 21st Century mandates that the human domains of SCIENCE, ART, LAW AND RELIGION come forth to defend, restore, heal, protect, secure and sustain our broken and at-risk civilization and humanity. THE ART OF MUSIC CAN PLAY GREAT ROLE. Let us begin today through the unleashing of our talents, gifts, potentials and blessings!

GOD INSPIRED ARTISTIC EXPRESSIONS
Theological Values for Human Redemption

1. Acculturation
2. Assimilation
3. Balance
4. Beauty
5. Civility
6. Compatibility
7. Complementary
8. Congruence
9. Continuity
10. Elevation
11. Elegance
12, Equality
13. Equilibrium
14. Goodness
15. Grace
16. Harmony
17. Humanitarianism
18. Joy
19. Justice
20. Kindness

21. Knowledge
22. Liberty
23. Love
24. Mediation
25. Order
26. Peace
27. Radiance
28. Reconciliation
29. Regeneration
30. Righteousness
31. Restoration
32. Resurrection
33. Serenity
34. Symmetry
35. Synchronization
36. Systemization
37. Transfiguration
38. Transformation
39. Transcendence
40. Truth

These elevating and transformative theological spiritual values can be expressed through human hearts, spirits, minds, personal service, families, agencies, institutions, culture and nations. They can be illustrated, demonstrated, transmitted and assimilated through the blessings of SCIENCE, ART, LAW AND THEOLOGY. These values give a picture beyond the reality of WHAT IS - TO WHAT OUGHT TO BE, AND

WHAT GOD HAS MADE POSSIBLE TO BE, AND CAN BE. EVERY PERSON IS INVITED TO EMBRACE THESE TRANSFORMATIVE ARTISTIC VALUES.

The Public Theologian

FOUNDATION MINISTRIES
Validation of Truth Through Public Theology
A Brief Synopsis

The Foundation Baptist Church was founded and established in June 1996 by Pastor W. J. Webb at Usher Elementary School in Atlanta, Georgia. W. J. Webb was a former minister and Interim Pastor at the Wheat Street Baptist Church upon the retirement of The Reverend William H. Borders in 1988. Foundation Baptist Church relocated to Summerset Assisted Living Community in Southwest Atlanta in 2002 and provided a unique ministry for the Summerset residents and persons from the outside community up to the time of the Covid 19 Pandemic that began about 2020. Subsequent to 2020, the Foundation continued to meet virtually with all of its worship and Christian educational activities.

In the year 2002, Pastor W. J. Webb incorporated three nonprofit charitable organizations, including Foundation Baptist Church through the State of Georgia. The Church was incorporated in order to become an officially registered legal entity to operate professionally as a church and business enterprise. Two other organizations grew out from the Foundation Baptist Church.

Christian Institute of Public Theology (CIPT):

The Christian Institute of Public Theology was incorporated in the year 2002 to provide relevant theological education, training, pastoral services, remedial treatment and training certifications. The Christian Institute is primarily a public theological education educational institution to train and educate theological students to become professional skilled human helpers and professional public theological practitioners. CIPT is not a membership organization. It is a 501, c3 nonprofit educational, treatment and training organization. CIPT, The Christian Institute of Public Theology has trained and certified hundreds of students, ministers and public theologians during its twenty-plus years of tenured operation. CIPT is eligible to receive public and private donations to carry out its mission as a charitable nonprofit corporation. It is designed to teach and equip its students with biblical-based truths, education, Christian values, skills and principles to ameliorate the escalating, unprecedent ed cultural crises of this 21st Century.

The Christian Association of Public Theologians (CAPT):

CAPT (Christian Association of Public Theologians) is a membership nonprofit charitable Christian organization incorporated in the State of Georgia in 2002, to provide education, and public advocacy, cultivate humanitarian associations, practice public theology in the development and implementation of public concerns and public policies in the interest of public health, public safety and the public good of society. The public theologians are the vanguards and exponents of truth, justice, freedom, survival values and humanitarian civility for all people. Public theologians embrace the concerns for needed societal reformation and transformation of agencies and institutions for law-abiding behavior, goodwill and peace in accordance with the will of God.

CAPT has hosted fifteen successful annual conferences under the leadership of the Reverend Pastor Melvin Ware. CAPT is challenged in many areas. It is challenged to increase its membership under the leadership of Foundation Worship leader Rev. Marleesha Carmichael, Along with Foundation's Pastoral Coordinator and Zoom Platform provider, Rev. Thomas Luke and other foundation ministers, Reverends; Dawn Robinson, Linda Perrin, Vernessa Hollis and ministers Karen Webb-Allen, Rodney Allen, Elder Nathaniel and Minister Christine Brown. Along with our other associated ministers and public theologians in the persons of Rev. Donnie Bell and Dr. Van Shrieves and our new members, we are encouraged to invite others and increase our membership and share this good news abroad, in the public square, neighborhoods, websites and internet. God has provided CAPT a significant opportunity to make a constructive and positive contribution to America and the world.

FOUNDATIONS FOR PUBLIC THEOLOGY:

The primary foundations for public theology are the Holy Bible, the Gospel of Jesus Christ and the validated knowledge of truth. Foundation Baptist Church provides a platform for the teaching and the practice of public theology in conjunction with the teaching, preaching, worshipping and pastoral care ministerial Christian services.

PUBLIC THEOLOGY VS. THE COMPLEX CULTURE CRISIS:

Public theology is an effort to "put on the whole armor of God." (Ephesians 6: 10-18). The fight against ignorance, evil and wickedness is not a simplistic endeavor. Public theology in acknowledging the complexities of the 21st Century culture crises, utilizes metaphorical language to highlight the complexities of our cultural crises and the precarious human predicament of the 21st Century.

CAPT and CIPT have set forth four metaphors to help in understanding the extraordinary needs in combatting and coping with the unprecedented complex problems of this 21st Century. Jesus often used parables to express great truths to make the meanings clearer. Metaphors are used similarly here to shed light on the complexities and the requirements to find the appropriate answers and solutions. The metaphors applied here denote complex academic disciplines to solve complex problems. The metaphors employed here are described as POLITICAL PHYSICS, SOCIAL CHEMISTRY, LEGAL MATHEMATICS AND THEOLOGICAL ETHICS.

POLITICAL PHYSICS is the study of human behavior, social actions, social interactions, group formations, and collective actions based on political and ideological belief systems, motivations and persuasions. Political physics studies the causes and realities of the motivations behind the behaviors and social actions in the body politics of societies. It studies the motivations of collective social behaviors and actions and communal decisions. Simple arithmetic is not sufficient to explain the social dynamics involved in political physics.

SOCIAL CHEMISTRY is the study of the dynamic behavioral impact of the heterogeneous associations, sentiments, socializations, co-operations, assimilations, dissociations of the mixtures of races, nationalities, ethnicities, religions, and other ideological belief systems. How can a representative responsible positive social consensus be achieved from these human heterogeneous individual and social mixtures? Chemistry is a complex academic discipline that studies the mixtures of a variety of substances, elements and chemicals under a variety of conditions. Some mixtures can be toxic and even lethal. Social chemistry provides an avenue of conceiving ways and means to make heterogeneous diverse social mixtures and human integration more homogeneous and healthier. The theological values of truth and love can add health to diverse human integration;

LEGAL MATHEMATICS is the study of the multiple intertwined laws that govern human behavior. Human beings are governed by natural laws, divine ins and manmade laws, and man-made statutory laws by local, state and federal governments. A type of legal mathematics is required to calculate the validity, congruence, equity and just application of these varied laws and circumstances of their application and imposition. Public theology helps to validate the truth, soundness, relevance and justice of these multiplicities of laws that often conflict with each other. The allocation of justice based on adjudicated merit is a prime value in human societies. These intricacies of the various governing laws are not always simple. It is mandatory that jurists and administrators of justice be acquainted with political physics, social chemistry, legal mathematics and theological ethics.

THEOLOGICAL ETHICS is the study of that which is validated as being true, righteous, just, moral, good and ethical according to divine creation and the revealed will of God, the Creator. Theological ethics must be based on universal principles to subscribe to a universal standard. It must answer the questions definitively: What is morally right? What is morally wrong? What is true? What is false? What is the universal standard for human moral and ethical conduct and behavior? What and who is the authority for human and moral standards? Public theology seeks to answer these questions for human civilization.

These foregoing metaphors are designed to provide an appreciation for the complexity of America's and humanity's unprecedented complex cultural crises and problems in the 21st Century AD. The Scriptures state that when Israel had no king, "every man did what was right in his own eyes." (Judges 21:25). Public Theology affirms that the loving God and the Creator of mankind, have provided sufficient values, standards and answers for mankind, even in the midst of the confused humanity of the 21st Century. These basic and core standards and values are found in abundance in the Word of God in the Holy Bible. The great duty and the great challenge for mankind is to SHARE THE WORD OF GOD IN THE HOLY BIBLE. HIS WORD WILL ACCOMPLISH IT:
PURPOSE AND NOT RETURN VOID. MAKE IT A TOP PRIORITY TC SHARE AND SPREAD GOD'S WORD TO YOUR NEIGHBOR AND THE WORLD. GOD HAS EVEN GIVEN A SAVIOR, JESUS CHRIST, WHO!
THE WAY, THE TRUTH AND THE LIFE!

FOUNDATION EDUCATING THE PEOPLE OF GOD

CREDIBLE MEANS OF VALIDATING TRUTH

Truth suggests an objectified reality-based existence. Truth is a quantifiable or substantive configuration of reality in the midst of transitory processes of the universe. Truth possesses an independent identifiable existence of its own. The identification of truth is critical for human life and human existence. The opposites or substitutes for truth are fictional, false, lies and deceptions. There are no substitutes for truth. Truth is that constant or stability that underlies the transitory and changing processes of the universe. Knowing the truth is critical for many reasons. To be ignorant of the truth is to be in bondage. Knowing the truth liberates you from bondage. Jesus said, "And ye shall know the truth and the truth shall make you free." (John 8:32)

The Christian Institute of Public Theology has devised and employed four ways or means to validate that which is true. As a theological foundational reference for validating the truth, a familiar Scriptural reference is used in (Matthew 5:15) where Jesus told his listeners, "You are the salt of the earth: but if the salt has lost his savour, wherewith shall it be salted?" Salt is a white crystalline substance found in natural beds in seawater. It is used for seasoning and preserving food. It is revealing that Jesus told his listeners that they are the salt of the earth. This parable or metaphor suggests that the followers of Jesus have a duty to be seasoners and preservers of the earth. Therefore, in order to get the full import of this metaphor of salt, an acronym based on SALT is developed to clarify and amplify the lessons of SALT as a valuable truism. The acronym derived from SALT is used as a method to validate truth.

Academic Branches of Learning

There are four primary branches of learning. They are known as SCIENCE, ART, LAW and THEOLOGY. The predominant degrees awarded from educational institutions fall in those four categories of science, art, law and theology. These degrees certify satisfactory completion of education and learning from these respective accredited educational institutions. The certified standards employed by these educational institutions have an underlying presumption that they are providing validated and universally truly recognized bodies of knowledge, professional skills and sound doctrines. The acronym of SALT is based on the foundations of these four branches of learning and education.

S.A.L.T. as an Acronym to Validate Truth

An acronym uses letters in a specific word to assign a word with a specific meaning by using each letter in the specific word. Each letter in the word SALT is used to express individual words beginning with each letter of SALT. Salt is a seasoner and preserver for food. Salt is used as a metaphor denoting the use and function of followers of Jesus for their roles for the earth (people of the) as compared to the role of SALT to season and preserve food. The use of the word salt is a metaphor to bring about a realization of a truth or an insight to help one realize a truth. The use of salt to season and preserve food is translated into the use of the followers of Jesus to season and preserve the earth for the enjoyment and sustenance of life for mankind.

SALT

The	S	in	(S)ALT	represents	SCIENCE
The	A	in	S(A)LT	represents	ART
The	L	in	SA(L)T	represents	LAW
The	T	in	SAL(T)	represents	THEOLOGY

Science, Art, Law and Theology represent professionally recognized branches of knowledge that can be used to validate that which is true. Truth can be validated by the balance, synchronization and harmony of art. Truth can be validated by the mandates, dictates and prelates of law. Truth can be validated by God's creation, revelations, transformations and Biblical Salvation.

These four methods of validating the truth can be illustrated, demonstrated and expressed scientifically, artistically, legalistically and theistically. This knowledge wisdom and understanding are available in abundance. There is no plausible excuse for ignorance. The educators, artists, jurists and theologians have a special responsibility in educating the people of God, of America and of the world.

Hosea has given the warning that humanity perishes for lack of knowledge. God gives mankind a clear direction in Jesus Christ, who said,, "I am the way, the truth and the life, no man cometh unto the Father but by me." (John 14:6). There is one God, one Savior, one Bible and one humanity.

INITIATIVES FOR RESTORING CULTURAL VALUES
Tach and Practice the Governing Creeds of America

The governing creeds of America include the Bible; the Declaration of Independence, the U.S. Constitution, Pledge of Allegiance to One Nation Under God. In God We Trust and Government of the people, for the people and by the people.)

The public theologians must take the initiative to facilitate the practice and the process of helping all American citizens to live up to the governing creeds of America in order to achieve the God-given human rights of life, liberty, pursuit of happiness, equal justice and equal protection of the laws enumerated in the Bible, American Creeds and the U.s. Constitution.

All Americans must be taught that A Nation Under God requires all citizens to be taught and learn about the knowledge and truth of God in the Holy Bible and the governing creeds of America.

RECOMMENDED INITIATIVES FOR PUBLIC THEOLOGIANS

1. Organize An Expansive Public Theology Membership Drive.
2. Publish and Distribute a Periodic Public Theologian News Letter.
3. Establish A School to Teach Public Theology. (The Institute of Public Theology).
4. Educate and Train Public Theologians as Professionals and Skilled Helpers.

5. Teach Theological Ethics. Foundations for Ethical Leadership and Professionalism.
6. Teach Values for Ethical Leadership and Business Professionalism.
7. Teach Values and Traits for Character Education.
8. Teach Public Theology and Public Policy Formulation.
9. Teach Ethical Values for Theological Leadership.
10. Teach God's Purpose and Salvation Plan for Mankind.
11. God's Way, Truth, Life and Favor for Mankind.
12. God's Will, Kingdom, Household of Faith on Earth and In Heaven.

RECOMMENDATIONS FOR THE PUBLIC GOOD:
Adopt Merit Systems as opposed to "Buddy Systems."
Avoid electing unethical & biblically illiterate leaders.
Avoid public representatives with conflicts of interest.

Educational References:

The Bible, James Strong Concordance, US Constitution, Declaration of Independence, Pledge of Allegiance, US Motto (In God We Trust), The Way Out of Darkness-Vital Public Theology (W. J. Webb); A Table of Visions to Revive the Nation (W.J. Webb),

THE EMPOWERMENT OF BLACK AMERICAN MUSIC
The Music that Heals and Gives Hope
The Christian Institute of Public Theology

Black American music from its beginning in the 17th Century healed, elevated; motivated, inspired and gave hope to downtrodden people. This fine elevating soothing elevating art of the soul played a significant role in the survival of a suppressed people with no earthly hope. This music of the soul of the Black American enslaved Negro elevated their spirits from the lowest depths of depression to the highest peaks of hope. Their music was their primary therapy. It was through their music that they expressed their disappointments, pain, heartaches, heartbreaks and sorrows. They also used music to express their jubilations and joys. They expressed artistic sounds that articulated a peculiar language that originated from the sentiments of their souls. In addition to the lyrics and melody, they would express their music through moaning and groaning, humming and whistling.

The significant role of the great empowering Black American music must be revisited for the education, elevation and the inspiration for human survival, civilization, cultural enrichment and humanitarian refinements. Great lessons of life, survival and endurance are derived from Black American music. The great melodies, educational and enlightening lyrics kept the suppressed Black Americans mentally, morally and spiritually alive. They learned to sing when they were happy and when they were sad. They learned to incorporate and translate their sorrows and sadness; their pains and heartbreaks into music. Their predominant hope and inspiration came from their belief in God, the Bible and Jesus Christ.

The oppressed Black Americans had great ethical and biblical themes to sing about. Their musical themes were based on their faith in a loving, forgiving, just, righteous and merciful God. Many of their themes were taken directly from Scripture. In spite of their enslavement and suffering, they put their faith and hope in the loving, forgiving and merciful God. Therefore, they had something significant to sing about in the midst of all of their joys and sorrows. These great inexhaustible ethical, moral and biblical themes provided a message of hope, Faith, love and healing to sing about in every human situation they found themselves.

Black American music permeates the American culture; especially the Black American culture. On-screen, sports and entertainment arenas. Blac American music has been commonplace in churches, schools and homes. the early development of Black American music, it pervaded Black American culture. The Black Americans sang in the cotton fields and corn fields. They sang as they worked on railroads highways and bridges. They sang as they cut down trees and hauled logs. They sang as they ginned and bailed cost Many of them sang, whistled, blew the harmonica and played the guitar they walked up and down unpaved roads in the middle of the night. T. learned to transform sound into a joyful noise and hymns of healing: peace. Through music, the Black American found transcendent joy and peace in the midst of injustice and hostility.

AMERICAN CITIZENS FOR BIBLE SCHOOL CURRICULUM A PETITION TO US STATE GOVERNORS

(The Public Theologians)

AS AN AMERICAN CITIZEN AND CITIZENS OF THE STATE OF _____, I _____. WE _____HEREBY PETITION GOVERNOR _____ AND THE STATE DEPARTMENT TO EXPEDITIOUSLY, ADOPT THE BIBLICAL CURRICULUM IN ALL PUBLIC SCHOOLS FROM K-12 AS HISTORY AND LITERATURE BASED ON THE NATIONAL COUNCIL ON BIBLE CURRICULUM IN PUBLIC SCHOOLS AS A PRIORITY WITHOUT DELAY. (NOTE: This Bible Curriculum is not for the purpose of religion, worship or proselytizing) IT IS FOR THE PURPOSE OF THE KNOWLEDGE, EDUCATION OF THE HISTORY AND LITERATURE OF THE BIBLE.

PETITIONERS

NAME OF CITIZEN OR ORGANIZATION	CONTACT(OPTIONAL)
1.	
2.	
3.	
4.	
5.	
6.	
7.	
8.	
9.	
10.	

AMERICAN CITIZENS FOR BIBLE SCHOOL CURRICULUM A PETITION FOR US STATE GOVERNORS

PETITIONERS

NAME OF CITIZEN OR ORGANIZATION	CONTACT(OPTIONAL)
1.	
2.	
3.	
4.	
5.	
6.	
7.	
8.	
9.	
10.	
11.	
12.	
13.	
14.	
15.	

THE PUBLIC THEOLOGIANS